Dedication

Incredibly Gifted has been written out of the years of my study of the Word of God while I ministered to people as their pastor or leader in evangelism. The principles and concepts I have set forth have been tried and tested through the lives of these wonderful people.

Many were comfortable in serving in the area of their giftedness but believed that they could never be effective as personal witnesses for Christ. Often, they were bound with fear. But they responded to my encouragement and challenge to allow me to equip them to share Christ and to lead others to know Him. They were willing to allow God to use the uniqueness of their personalities and particular gifts to share Christ in a natural and non-threatening way. Through their witness, Christ has been glorified, people have come to know him as Savior and Lord, and joy has filled their own lives.

Some who did not know Christ accepted Him and committed their lives to be his witnesses when they realized God's wonderful purpose for them to be on mission for Him. They, like Paul, began immediately to use their gifts to effectively share Christ with others.

Therefore, to these committed and courageous Believers, my friends and loved ones, I dedicate this book. It is my prayer that through the understanding of the biblical principles in this book, multitudes of others will realize that they, too, can effectively share Jesus through the use of their gifts.

D1113807

Foreword

Several things are absolutely crystal clear in the Word of God. The first thing that is crystal clear is that one can only be saved and go to Heaven through faith in the Lord Jesus Christ. The second thing that is absolutely clear is that every Christian has been given spiritual gifts to carry out the tasks that God has given each of us to do. The third thing that is crystal clear is that like the Lord Jesus Himself, we are to "seek and to save that which is lost."

Darrell Robinson has put those three truths together in a marvelous book entitled *Incredibly Gifted*. His thesis is simple—whatever special gifts God has given to you, these gifts can be used, should be used, indeed must be used to fulfill the Great Commission and bring people to a saving knowledge of Jesus Christ.

Many books are written on spiritual gifts. Many books are written on evangelism. To my knowledge, this is the first book I have ever seen that instructs us in a practical way on how we can use each spiritual gift to fulfill the Great Commission and bring people to a saving knowledge of Jesus Christ.

My friend and brother, Darrell Robinson, who is one of the greatest personal soul-winners I've ever met, has done the kingdom of God, as well as the church, a favor by writing this book. It will bless you, change you, and motivate you to use all that God has given you to bring people to His son, Jesus Christ. I encourage every Christian to read it again and again!

James Merritt, Senior Pastor
First Baptist Church
Snellville, Georgia

Foreword

God has given Darrell Robinson the unique ability to bring to us a clear and deeper understanding of the reason God has endowed the Body of Christ with spiritual gifts. In this book, you will see that these gifts have been built into us by God—made a part of us—to be used for the benefit of others and, ultimately, for God's glory.

Johnny Hunt, Pastor
First Baptist Church
Woodstock, Georgia

About the Author

Darrell W. Robinson has a rich and varied background in ministry. He now serves as president of Total Church Life Ministries, Inc. and ministers both nationally and internationally. This ministry assists local churches, associations, states, and national Christian bodies in strategic evangelism and missions.

Robinson also serves as professor of evangelism at Luther Rice Seminary.

He received his education at Baylor University, Southwestern Baptist Theological Seminary, and Luther Rice Seminary, where he earned a Doctor of Ministry degree. He was awarded honorary doctorates by Houston Baptist University and Minnesota Graduate School of Theology.

During a 35-year period, Robinson served as pastor of several churches in Texas, Kansas, and Alabama. Every church under his pastoral leadership experienced exceptional growth through effective evangelism and discipleship. He modeled in his churches the principles he shares in this book about spiritual gifts. His pastorates included helping start two new churches—Midway Baptist Church in Big Spring, Texas, and Berea Baptist Church in Big Spring, Texas. Other churches in which he served as pastor are First Baptist, Liberal, Kansas; First Baptist, Vernon, Texas; First Baptist, Pasadena, Texas; and Dauphin Way Baptist, Mobile, Alabama.

Robinson is widely known as an evangelist, equipper of pastors, and conference speaker. He served as vice president for evangelism of the Southern Baptist Convention's Home Mission Board between 1989 and 1997. Then, following a convention reorganization, he served with the SBC's North American Mission Board, from 1997 to 2000.

Through his work as a pastor, author, and evangelist, he has had international influence for evangelism and discipleship. His strategic evangelism and equipping materials have been used in Brazil, Korea, Romania, Croatia, Guyana, England, the Caribbean Islands, and other countries. He has been elected to numerous offices in the SBC.

Total Church Life, written by Robinson, is a strategy for evangelistic ministry that has been utilized by thousands of churches worldwide. He has also written *People Sharing Jesus*, which is used interdenominationally to train believers in a natural, non-threatening approach for witnessing, and the *Doctrine of Salvation*, a study to help ground believers in the faith. To help believers grow, he has written *What's Next?*

A native West Texan, Robinson grew up in Howard County and graduated from Coahoma High School, where he received honors in football and livestock work. He surrendered to preach at age 17 and began his first pastorate at age 18. Robinson and his wife, Kathleen, from the Brookhaven, Mississippi, area, have four children: Duane, a banker in Gladewater, Texas; Lori Winston, a Christian psychologist in The Woodlands, Texas; Robin Robinson, a pastor in Palatine, Illinois; and Loren Robinson, a church planter in New Palestine Indiana. The Robinsons have seven grandchildren: Matthew, Blakely, Kimberly, Natalie, Olivia, and Tabitha Robinson, and Katie and Christian Winston.

Table of Contents

Introduction

Great Commission Gifts

"What is your gift?" is a popular question among believers today. It is part of a long-term trend in which historically some facet of biblical truth periodically re-emerges to prominence. When this occurs, it brings a new and powerful dimension into the life of Christ's church. It might have been an almost-forgotten or much-neglected part of the God's truth. But, it becomes so prominent that it seems almost everyone is eventually talking and/or writing about it. For some, this trend becomes little more than a religious fad which they believe they must experience. God seems to work in this way to overcome and compensate for the neglect of facets of spiritual truth and areas of weakness in His church.

Discussions about spiritual gifts have become much like this. In recent years, considerable attention has been given to these gifts. Multitudes of books have been written on the subject. "Gift Inventories" and "Gift Assessments" techniques and materials have been developed to help individuals discover their spiritual gifts.

This greater emphasis on spiritual gifts has had a positive effect on believers individually. It has helped many people realize the importance of spiritual gifts in the body of Christ and to the work of the Kingdom. The spotlight on gifts has been positive for the church corporately, and it has helped to involve more believers in ministry and witness.

However, using a cerebral approach alone to determine a person's gifts has its shortcomings. Introspectively attempting to assess our spiritual gifts may prove to be exciting, entertaining, and enjoyable. I have personally done several gift studies, and I have enjoyed both filling out the "gift discovery" questionnaires and also discussing what my gifts seem to be. Gift studies and speculation about what our gifts are add some understanding and interest. But sadly, such activities seldom result in believers getting involved in exercising their gifts. *What really makes the difference* is practical involvement in the laboratory of the Body-Life of the church through obedience to Christ. Gift inventories and analyses are often subjective and introverted. They sometimes lead to abuse when people overemphasize their gift or refuse to meet a need because they don't have a particular gift. That approach to gifts then becomes a barrier to what God wants to do through us.

One member, named Jean, moved to a new area and joined the church in the community. She had served Christ for many years quietly in the background through ministries in her church. She knew she had the gift of ministry but certainly not of leadership. Soon she became aware of many older people who had special needs but were somewhat overlooked by the church. She spoke to the pastor about the need. The pastor asked Jean to start a ministry to senior adults and homebound persons.

Her response was, "I just want to be involved! I am not a leader! I do not have that gift."

The pastor said, "I believe you can do it, and I will help you. This is a real need within our church."

The pastor did help her get started. Her program became tremendously successful. Now it is a flourishing ministry. Jean found herself involved in using gifts she never knew she possessed. She used the gift of <u>administration and leadership</u> to enlist others to help, organize, and plan this ministry. She used the gifts of <u>mercy, giving, hospitality, exhortation,</u> and <u>teaching</u> in meeting the needs she observed. Through obedience to the Holy Spirit, she discovered multiple gifts by simply seeing a need and obeying Christ to help meet it.

OBEDIENCE IS THE KEY! It unlocked the door to Jean's gifts. To simply step out by faith to be available and obey Christ was the critical factor. To obey Him in the life of the church, His Body, both in ministry and witness, is the greatest adventure we can know. As we do, God will surface any and every gift needed for His body to accomplish what He wants done to fulfill His mission. Believers have the potential to have any gift, because of the One who lives in us is the source of those gifts. Christ is the perfect person. He possesses every gift. Through Him we can do all things (Phil. 4:13).

The major Bible passages about spiritual gifts are given in the context of discussions about the Body-Life of the church. They show that every gift has been given to enable the Body to function with health and effectiveness in fulfilling the Great Commission. *Our sovereign Lord has given every gift through individual believers to the Body of Christ for the building up of the body to fulfill the Great Commission; therefore, EVERY GIFT IS FOR EVANGELISM.*

The purpose of this book is to help individual believers and churches to obey Christ confidently and to move with Him on His mission. We will take a *fresh, biblical approach* to the study of spiritual gifts. We will look at biblical truths regarding when these gifts are given and what God will do as we trust and obey Him.

Chapter One

The Gifted Body of Christ

Outline

God has given spiritual gifts to the Body of Christ to build up the Body so it can fulfill the mission of Christ. Every member has gifts to use in teamship with other members to exalt the Savior, equip the saints, and evangelize the sinner.

I. The Nature of the Body
- Church Is People, Not Buildings
- Church Is the "Called Out Ones"
- Church Has Two Parts: Head and Body
- Church Has Two Perspectives: Gathered and Scattered

II. The Health of the Body
- The Unity of the Body. 1 Cor. 12:1-13
  The Key to Unity is the Headship of Christ
  The Attainment of Unity is through the Baptism of the
     Holy Spirit
- The Diversity within the Body. 1 Cor. 12:14-31
  Diversity Is Difficult
  Diversity Is Dynamic

III. The Purpose of the Body
- The Vision of the Church—Be the Body of Christ
- The Mission of the Church—to Use Spiritual Gifts to:
  Exalt the Savior—Col. 1: 18
  Equip the Saints—Eph .14:11-12
  Evangelize the Sinner—Acts 1:8

Chapter One

The Gifted Body of Christ

You have spiritual gifts, but do you know to whom they belong? They belong to the Body of Christ. Spiritual gifts are given to the Body. Three major passages in the New Testament deal with the subject of spiritual gifts. All three are given in the context of emphasis on the corporate Body of Christ. Gifts are mentioned in other places but are more extensively dealt with in the context of three "Body-Life" passages—Romans 12, 1 Corinthians 12, and Ephesians 4:1-16. Different gifts are listed and truths are given about how each is to be utilized. Understanding and effectively utilizing spiritual gifts happens through the ministry and witness of local churches. In churches teamship develops, and in churches members use their gifts to complement one another in ministry.

The Nature of the Body (Col. 1:18)

The "Meaning of Church" needs to be rediscovered in the 21st century. We live in a world that has forgotten what church is all about. So have many members and churches. Members often treat the church like another civic or service club. They allocate a little time to attend an acceptable number of meetings, give a little money like they are paying their dues, and occasionally do some kind of service project. They treat church the same way. It is simply another of many activities or organizations they add to their schedule.

But, church is not something we attend! It is who we are. WE CHRISTIANS ARE THE CHURCH! Church is people. It is not buildings. Nor is it organizations. It is people—people who have received Jesus Christ into their lives as Lord and Savior. Church is people who share Christ in fellowship with one another. It is people who share Him with those who are lost. Church is "People Sharing Jesus!"

In the New Testament the Greek word for church is *ekklesia*. It is a compound word made up of *ek,* a preposition that means "out of" and a noun, *kaleo,* meaning "to call". Church is "the called out ones." Church is people who have been called out from sin to salvation, from death to life, from hell to heaven, from slavery to Satan to service to the Savior.

The word *church* is used 115 times in the New Testament. It is used in a "general, spiritual, or invisible" sense 20 times. In those instances it refers to every believer regardless of denomination, location, or time. It is those who have been born again and who will meet Christ in the air and who will be with Him forever when He comes again.

Far more often *ekklesia* is used to refer to local churches (95 times). Writing to local churches Paul addressed the church at Corinth and the churches (plural) in Galatia. Jesus instructed John to write to the seven churches (plural) in Asia. Local churches are primary in the work of the Kingdom of God. They attempt to give visible, practical expression to the body of Christ through worshipping, fellowshipping, equipping, ministering, and evangelizing—all forms of carrying out the Great Commission. Every local church is an individual body with Christ as its Head. And each church is a gifted body, too. It is gifted by the Holy Spirit to fulfill the mission of its Head, the Lord Jesus Christ. Gifts are distributed through the lives of members of the body.

An analogy with a human body has been used throughout the Scripture to reveal the relationship between Christ and His church. A church like a human has two parts: head and body. The head is none other than Jesus Christ, the Son of God. The body is made up of the many members bound together in unity under His Headship.

"And He is the head of the body, the church, who is the beginning, the firstborn from the dead, that in all things He may have the preeminence" (Col. 1:18).

He is Head! We are the body! Never forget who is what in church! Christ is Head, and He has preeminence. We are the body, and no member or members of the body can be head. Jesus is Head! He will tolerate no rival. When someone or some group lifts up themselves and rivals Jesus for headship, the fellowship will be disrupted, and the body will become dysfunctional. Jesus will tolerate no rival for Headship in His body. He is to be lifted up and exalted by the body.

What is the significance of the *body* concept of the church? Why the analogy? 2 Corinthians 5 holds the key to understanding it. Our human body is called an earthly tent or tabernacle. It is a temporary "house" in which a believer lives. But one day the believer will move out into a "house not made with hands, eternal in the heavens." At the present time, however, this body houses not only the believer, but it also houses Jesus.

Our bodies as believers are not only the houses in which we live. They are the dwelling places of Christ who comes to "dwell in your hearts by faith" (Eph. 3:17). Individually and collectively we are the body of Christ! He lives in us. The body of Christ is dynamically filled with His life.

What tremendous potential! It is "Christ in you, the hope of glory" (Col.1:27). Every member has spiritual gifts given for the edification of the body. The body of Christ collectively possesses all the spiritual gifts of its members and is filled with Christ Himself.

As a body of Christ, a local church has <u>two perspectives</u>:

1. It is the church gathered; and
2. It is the church scattered!

On Sunday morning the church is *gathered* for worship, fellowship, prayer, teaching, equipping, etc. On Monday through Saturday the church is *scattered* for witness and ministry. Everywhere we go as Believers, Jesus goes in us and through us to do again all He did when He was here in the flesh! He is here in us. He is in us where we live, work, and play every day—in offices, plants, factories, schools, farms, ranches, hospitals, and neighborhoods. He is in us, loving people, touching people, ministering to people, and bringing people to God. Every gift given to each member individually and to the body collectively belongs to Jesus to be used to build up the Body and reach the lost.

The Health of the Body

Maximum utilization of spiritual gifts happens when a healthy body functions to fulfill the mission of Christ. Healthy bodies are strong. They grow! The question immediately arises, "What makes a church healthy? How can a body have and maintain good health?" There are two great essentials for the church body to be healthy and for the spiritual gifts of its members to be utilized meaningfully and effectively. These two essentials are seen in the outline of 1 Corinthians 12, one of the primary biblical passages on spiritual gifts which gives key principles for the body-life and health of a church:

First, unity must exist within the body (1 Cor. 12:1-13).

Second, diversity of members must exist in the body (1 Cor. 12:14-31).

The Unity of Members within the Body (1 Cor. 12:1-13)

God has given every church all it needs to do everything God wants it to do. He has set every member in the body "just as He pleased" (v. 18) and has given gifts "for the profit of all" (v. 7). The primary issue is that members function together in unity as one body.

The Headship of Christ is the key to unity. As each member lifts up Christ, the Head, and obeys Him, the members are drawn together in unity. As Head, He is the control-center. He directs every member. He coordinates the members, enabling them to function together *cooperatively* complementing one another. He gives gifts to every member to be used "for the profit of all" (1 Cor. 12:7). He directs their use so that through mighty power the body accomplishes His purpose.

Members of the body are to avoid two extremes in attitudes (Rom. 12:3). First, avoid an attitude of depreciating themselves. Otherwise feelings of inferiority will cause them to drop out in discouragement and stop participating in the life of the body. Second, avoid an attitude of superiority which depreciates other members. Otherwise, the body will become disunited and dysfunctional. Paul hilariously engages his imagination to show what would happen if members of a human body became competitive, quarrelsome, and refused to live and work in unity. He imagines the foot saying,

"Because I am not a hand, I am not of the body" (1 Cor. 12:15); and the ear says, "Because I am not an eye, I am not of the body" (vs. 16); "If the whole were an eye, where would be the hearing?" (v. 17).

What if my right foot decides during the night, "Darrell does not appreciate me! All I do is get walked on! And he puts me in a tight, smelly, old shoe! I wish I were a hand. The hand gets to do the good things. It combs his hair, brushes his teeth, and puts good smelling lotion on his face when he shaves. And all I get is walked on! I am going to quit! I resign! I am not going to work anymore!"

Morning comes and, unaware of what my foot decided, I get up, step down, and start to walk across the floor. And I fall flat on my face! My foot is not working! It has made my body a cripple! This happens in church. It is important that every member have a vital union with the Head and unity with the rest of the body.

Suppose my ear begins to feel unappreciated. It develops a low self-esteem comparing itself with the eye. The ear says, "The eye is so beautiful! People are always complimenting the eye. Nobody ever says, 'What a lovely ear.' All I ever do is stick out, and some people laugh at me. I am the first member of the body to get cold! I am not important! I am quitting! I am not going to hear anymore."

On the other hand, the eye cannot say to the hand, "I have no need of you" (vs. 21). The eye cannot be everything. What if the whole body were an eye? Just one big eye, rolling along through life! What a grotesque thing!

No one member can be the entire body. Every member is needed. EVERYBODY IS SOMEBODY IN THE LORD'S BODY!

When the members of the church use their spiritual gifts in cooperation and unity, the Body becomes <u>focused</u> on the mission of the Head. Concentration makes the body powerfully effective. God's ideal is for members of the body to use their spiritual gifts in teamship with one another rather than each working in isolation. Unity is essential to a healthy, growing body.

Unity is attained through the work of the Holy Spirit, who gives spiritual gifts. The Holy Spirit baptizes every member into union with Christ and into unity with one another. It happens at the time of a person's life-changing experience through Jesus Christ. It happens not to a select few who have a particular spiritual gift. It happens to every true born-again believer. The baptism of the Holy Spirit brings diverse members into spiritual unity. The church body is a living organism with spiritual life and unity, rather than an organization with well-oiled machinery. The church uses organization. It organizes its members to function effectively, but the church is an organism. Individual members maintain their diversity while living in spiritual unity and mutual concern for one another.

The Diversity of Members within the Body (1 Cor. 12:14-31)

Each member is different from every other member and functions in different ways, using his or her spiritual gifts to meet different needs for the mutual benefit of one another and for the edification of the body.

<u>Diversity is Difficult!</u> We tend to press everyone into the same mold rather than accepting each as God made him or her. Accepting the individuality of each member is primary for empowering the Body. Christ, the Head, desires for us to support and encourage one another in the use of our gifts.

Diversity is also difficult because we tend to depreciate ourselves. We sometimes fail to realize our own importance to the body. God wants to use each of us and each of our gifts. "For I say, through the grace given to me, to everyone who is among you, not to think of himself more highly than he ought to think, but to think soberly, as God has dealt to each one a measure of faith" (Rom. 12:3).

When the body of Christ practices the love of Christ, it reaches out and loves unconditionally all kinds of people. People with all types of problems are attracted by such a climate of love. In the world they face rejection and hostility. But in the church they find acceptance and support. For 35 years, I was pastor to lots of different people—long enough that I was pastor to some weirdos in my time.

One of those was Jimmy, a bill collector. That is how I got acquainted with him. Jimmy went to a door to collect for a bill. The debtor invited him in at the point of a pistol. According to Jimmy's story, the man put a pistol in his mouth and began to snap the trigger. It did not fire! He tied Jimmy and beat him, then left him alone in the house. Jimmy freed himself and went to the hospital, where I met him. He was ready to be saved! He came to church, confessed Christ, was baptized and started to Sunday School. He disrupted every Bible class he attended. Finally, he came to the Pastor's Bible Class. One Sunday I taught what the Bible says about tithing. Jimmy immediately began to tithe.

About a month later he came by my office to tell me he wanted his money back. He said, "You told me if I would tithe, God would bless me. I have been tithing for a month and God has not blessed me. I want my money back."

I said, "Jimmy, let me tell you how it works. When you give, the money is deposited in the bank. The church has a budget to determine how the money is to be spent. The church treasurer can write checks for what is covered by the budget. It is not in the budget to give it back to you. But, if you will be in church on Wednesday night, you may tell the church what you told me, and I am sure they will vote to give it back to you."

Jimmy said, "Forget it! That is all right!"

We talked about tithing. He studied the Scripture and continued to tithe. He was a different kind of guy. Another pastor observed him and said one day, "I wouldn't waste my time with a weirdo like him."

But, God uses weirdos too! There were times when I would put on my jeans and jacket and walk the streets with Jimmy witnessing to street people on drugs, alcohol, and with other problems. He led many to Christ and helped them begin to grow and follow Christ in the church. God uses all kinds of people! God even uses people we call *weirdos*. Every believer has gifts God wants to use in the body. The ministry and witness of the body for Christ is diminished when we exclude those who do not fit the mold we have unconsciously developed.

EVERYBODY IS SOMEBODY IN THE LORD'S BODY!

Diversity is Dynamic. Diversity is the dynamic of the church providing great potential for ministry and witness. God has made every member different with different gifts so He can use each in a different way to reach different kinds of people who need to know Christ. Diversity makes the church exciting and joyful. Members can be taught that in their uniqueness, they are valuable to God and to the church. We all have gifts to be used for His glory and praise. As every member is involved using his or her gifts in ministry and witness, the needs of the church and individual members will be met. Caring ministry to the lost of the community will be accomplished. It will open the door for a powerful witness for Christ. The challenge is every-member involvement. *The church must organize, enlist, and equip all members to use their gifts.*

It is a source of great joy when believers accept their individuality and realize God created them for a purpose and has given them gifts to accomplish their purpose. Many believers have no idea of this great truth. They become defeated and depressed with low self-esteem—yearning for direction in life but having no real compelling purpose. They need to be taught the Word of God, guided into an understanding of how God can work in their lives. Believers need to be encouraged and equipped "for the work of ministry" (Eph. 4:12).

Dessie was just such a person. The first time I saw her, she sat alone in church with her head down, appearing to be defeated and depressed. She was a drab, doormat sort of woman. I do not know how she got that way. I don't know if she had always been like that or if she had been beaten down by life's experiences so that she had no confidence and self-esteem.

Our Women's Missions director intentionally became acquainted with Dessie. She spent time with Dessie and asked her to go with her on evangelistic visits. With encouragement, she participated in the church's witness-training seminar. Dessie helped lead someone to Christ. With anxiety that caused her voice to tremble, she stood and shared about the experience in a large Bible class. Later, she gave her testimony about her own conversion experience. Dessie began to radiate the love and grace of Jesus. The drab, depressed little lady became a beautiful, radiant woman. She discovered her gift of ministry by getting involved in personal witnessing. Other gifts surfaced in her life.

Many members sit back and think they can do nothing and are worthless because they compare themselves with others and conclude they cannot do what those "outstanding people" are doing. As they are enlisted, equipped, involved, and encouraged by spiritual leaders and other members of the body, they will literally be transformed. They will experience God's using them and their gifts in ministry and witness for His glory, for the building up of the Body and for helping others. Involved believers are fulfilled and happy believers. Indeed, diversity is the dynamic of the church.

The Purpose of the Body

The question of the ages is, "What is the purpose of the church?" Since our Lord founded the church, it has been driven by varied purposes. At times political agendas have dominated its interests; at other times human welfare has been its driving passion; still in other times education and social issues have been its underlying purpose. The real question is, "What was the intention of the founder, our Lord Jesus Christ?"

The Vision of the Church comes from its Head, Jesus Christ. Jesus said, "On this rock I will build My church, and the gates of Hades shall not prevail against it" (Matt. 16:18). "And He is the head of the body, the church, who is the beginning, the firstborn from the dead, that in all things He may have the preeminence" (Col. 1:18). Like in a human body, in the body of Christ, the head has vision.

What should be the vision of a church, according to New Testament principles? Very simple! Our vision as a church is to **be the Body of Christ** with all that implies. It means that we will corporately and individually live under His authority and Lordship. He is our head. We will live in unity with each other because we have the same Head and Lord. All of our gifts and abilities are under His control and are available to Him. We will live in obedience to Him as He directs our lives individually and our church corporately. We are His Body and will do what He came to do. We will carry out His mission in our community and world.

The Mission of the Church as the Body of Christ is three-fold:
EXALT THE SAVIOR,
EQUIP THE SAINTS, AND
EVANGELIZE THE SINNER
This three-faceted mission builds a balanced church life as is pointed out extensively in my previous book, *Total Church Life*, published by Broadman & Holman Publishers. A church cannot do one of these without doing all three. If we think we can, we are deceiving ourselves.

Dr. Ted Ward, outstanding missiologist and professor at Trinity Evangelical Divinity School, Deerfield, Illinois, said, "This mission statement has it all together. Do not ever stop doing this. You have it in the right order: Exalt, Equip, Evangelize. But, you do it simultaneously."

Every spiritual gift in the life of every member is needed to fulfill a church's mission. Members function as a team with each having a part in making up of the whole, complementing and strengthening each other as they focus on the priority of exalting the Savior, equipping the saints, and evangelizing the sinner.

A New Testament church is on mission to exalt the Savior! He is Lord! Head of the body! "In all things He has the preeminence" (Col. 1:18). Jesus said, "If I be lifted up, I will draw all men to me" (John 12:32). A true church is one that lifts Him up in Lordship and obedience, in praise and worship, in unity and fellowship, and in organization and administration. Through prayer and love the Body of Christ is filled with the Spirit and is empowered by this vital union.

As Christ is lifted up, His life fills the Body with the dynamic of His indwelling presence. He unifies the members so the church can equip the saints. "And He Himself gave some to be apostles, some prophets, some evangelists, some pastors and teachers, for the equipping of the saints for the work of ministry, for the edifying of the Body of Christ" (Eph. 4:11-12). Members with leadership gifts equip and train other members to use their spiritual gifts effectively in building up the body in maturity through ministry and discipleship and in number through evangelistic outreach.

When members of the Body are being equipped and are exalting the Savior by obediently following Him, evangelism happens! A healthy Body will be doing what its Head, the Lord Jesus, came to do. He said, "The Son of Man has come to seek and to save that which was lost" (Luke 19:10). In a healthy, obedient Body of Christ, every believer will be involved in using his or her gifts to evangelize those who are lost.

A healthy church will obey Jesus in His strategy to reach every person with the gospel. Christ gave His strategy in Acts 1:8, "But you shall receive power when the Holy Spirit has come upon you, and you shall be witnesses to Me in Jerusalem, and in all Judea and Samaria, and to the end of the earth."

This is a strategy of Total Evangelism. This biblical strategy is examined in detail in *Total Church Life*, Chapters 9-13. Jesus' strategy will involve a local church in Total Penetration of its area with the gospel, sharing Jesus with every person, and not overlooking anyone. Total Penetration requires Total Participation of the members of the church. It means that members of the church will be equipped to share Christ with each person in such a way that he or she can respond to Christ with understanding. A one-time saturation project is not enough. It must be an on-going process of repeatedly sharing Him with every lost and unchurched person until each has come to know and follow Him.

To implement this exciting and practical strategy demands Total Participation of the church's membership in witness. The pastor and leaders cannot do it alone. It requires every believer. Believers must be enlisted and equipped to use their gifts to witness to those who need Christ. Every gift can be used to share Christ, lead the lost to Him, and disciple them.

All the spiritual gifts are to be used in some way to exalt the Savior. They will be involved in equipping the saints for the work of ministry. Every gift will be involved in evangelizing the sinner. Thus, the mission of Christ will be fulfilled through His gifted Body!

All the members of a church body with their gifts complement one another to make up a whole and powerful body. The gifted members functioning in unity become a powerful team to accomplish the purpose of the Head, Jesus Christ!

APPLICATION

What percentage of your church's membership truly understands what church is?

_____

_____

_____

How can you help your members understand the nature of the church and truly be the church?

_____

_____

_____

What can your church members do to be the church as they scatter to where they live, work, and play?

_____

_____

_____

How would you diagnose your church's spiritual health?

_____

_____

_____

What can your church do to fulfill Jesus' strategy of evangelizing its area?

_____

_____

_____

Chapter Two

God's Power Formula
Outline

The Holy Spirit is primary in the use of spiritual gifts. The Holy Spirit is God's Salvation Gift. Five transactions of the Holy Spirit are as follows:

I. The Birth of the Spirit John 3:1-18
   - The New Birth Is a Mystery
   - The New Birth Is a Miracle

II. The Baptism of the Holy Spirit 1 Cor. 12:13
   - Union with Jesus
   - Unity with the Body

III. The Indwelling Of the Holy Spirit 1 Cor. 6:19-20
   - Indwells the Corporate Body
   - Indwells the Individual Believer

IV. The Sealing of the Holy Spirit Eph. 1:13-14; 4:30
   The Sealing of the Holy Spirit suggests the following:
   - A Guarantee
   - A Stamp
   - A Designation
   - A Brand

V. Filled with The Holy Spirit Eph. 5:18; Acts 4:31 Filling Suggests the Control of the Holy Spirit
   - A Command
   - An Act of God
   - A Continuing Action

Chapter Two

God's Power Formula

The Holy Spirit is our "salvation gift." He is God in us to empower our spiritual gifts. God has enabled us to live in the fullness of His power! The Holy Spirit is God's power formula for our spiritual lives!

The Holy Spirit arranges spiritual gifts in the Body and enables individual believers and the corporate Body of Christ for its mission. One of the biblical lists of spiritual gifts is in 1 Corinthians 12, where verse 11 says, "But one and the same Spirit works all these things, distributing (spiritual gifts) to each one individually as He wills." He both distributes spiritual gifts and empowers believers and churches to use them for the glory of God and for the mission of Christ.

To be effective in the utilization of spiritual gifts, we need to understand who the Holy Spirit is and what He does. He is a Person, a Divine Person! The Holy Spirit is not an "it"! The Holy Spirit is "He"! A personal noun or pronoun is used when the Bible refers to the Holy Spirit. Jesus said, "I will pray the Father, and He will give you another Helper, that He may abide with you forever—the Spirit of truth, whom the world cannot receive, because it neither sees Him nor knows Him; but you know Him, for He dwells with you and will be in you" (John 14:16-17).

We Christians do not say, "The Force be with you." The Holy Spirit is not an impersonal force. He is a Divine Person, not a divine influence. He has the traits of personality: He loves, can be grieved, quenched, obeyed, loved, and followed. He is God—the Third Person of the Godhead! Through the Holy Spirit, God, the Father, and Jesus, the Son, are present not only with us, but also within us (John 14:14-18).

Without the Holy Spirit there is no gospel! God, the Father, so loved the world that He gave His only begotten Son, Jesus, so that we may be <u>born of the Holy Spirit</u> (John 3:3-18).

However, in a day of disobedient church members and dead churches, many are like the mighty Samson in Judges 16:20. With their heads on the lap of the Delilah of this world, shorn of their power, they awaken surrounded by the enemy, "but do not know that the Lord has departed from them."

A great Christian leader said, "The Holy Spirit could totally withdraw from many of our churches, and they would never know the difference. They would simply go on as usual!"

The Holy Spirit not only distributes spiritual gifts, but He is Himself The Gift. He is our salvation gift. When we are saved, we receive the Holy Spirit! "Then Peter said to them, 'Repent, and let every one of you be baptized in the name of Jesus Christ for the remission of sins; and you shall receive the gift of the Holy Spirit" (Acts 2:38).

As God's salvation gift to us, the Holy Spirit initiates five transactions in our lives. Through these five transactions, He empowers us to live the "Jesus-life" and to share Jesus with others. It is humanly impossible for us to live like Jesus. No one but Jesus can live like Jesus! The only possibility for us to live like Jesus is for Jesus to live like Jesus through the Holy Spirit within us!

The Holy Spirit initiates five transactions in us as we experience conversion. First, He transacts the new birth experience. Second, He baptizes us into the body of Christ. Third, He indwells us. Fourth, He seals us. Fifth, the Holy Spirit fills us.

Born of the Holy Spirit—John 3:1-18

Jesus said, "Unless one is born again, he cannot see the kingdom of God" (John 3:3). The physical or flesh-birth is not enough for one to be able to enter the kingdom of God. Every person must be born of the Holy Spirit. This birth is a <u>mystery</u>. It is like the wind blowing. We hear the sound of it. We feel it and see the evidences of it, but, we cannot explain where it comes from nor where it goes. But, we know the wind is blowing. The Holy Spirit is at work within us, and we see the evidences of His activity through changes of attitudes, desires, direction, and habits in our lives.

Through this spiritual birth we become a new creation in Christ (2 Cor. 5:17). This birth is a <u>miracle</u>. Jesus said, "That which is born of flesh is flesh and that which is born of the Spirit is spirit." By the physical birth we become children of a human family. That is not sufficient to become a part of the family of God. To become a part of the family of God, one must be born spiritually by the supernatural power of the Holy Spirit. It is an inner transformation!

An outstanding illustration is the testimony of Tom Skinner, a great African-American Christian who has now gone on to heaven. Tom grew up on the streets of New York City. He was tough and mean. He became president of the Harlem Lords, one of the most vicious street gangs. One night Tom was strategizing for a battle in a war with a rival gang. He turned on his radio to listen to music while he planned.

Much to his surprise, someone was speaking at the time music usually played! It was a preacher! Tom reached to turn off the radio just as the preacher read 1 Corinthians 5:17, "Therefore if any man is in Christ, he is a new creation; old things have passed away; behold, all things have become new." Tom was captivated by this word's power. He couldn't turn it off. The preacher asked listeners to pray in repentance and faith to receive Christ. Tom did!

The next day he stood before the Harlem Lords gang, resigned as president, told them he had become a new creation in Christ Jesus and that he had committed his life to Christ! Tom said that as he walked out, he fully expected a knife in his ribs. A person didn't resign from the Harlem Lords. He said that he had personally broken the legs of people who tried to resign. But, he walked out untouched!

Later, another gang leader told Tom that he had his hand on his switchblade and was about to stab him in his rib, but his hand paralyzed. He could not move his hand! That young man, too, turned to Christ and was saved. What a tremendou miracle! Tom Skinner became a mighty witness and voice for Christ across the world.

The life-changing experience with the Holy Spirit—called the new birth or being born again—means that all sin is forgiven and the believer has a new power to live for Christ. At the new birth, the Holy Spirit begins the work of enabling the believer to be fruitful and to use his or her spiritual gifts for the glory of God and for the mission and ministry of the Body of Christ.

Baptized by the Holy Spirit—1 Corinthians 12:13

The baptism of the Holy Spirit happens when a person is born again. It is a Holy Spirit transaction that happens at conversion. It is not the result of a subsequent, spiritual experience nor of spiritual growth. It is not the result of, nor is it in connection with, a person receiving any particular spiritual gift. "For by one Spirit we were all baptized into one body—whether Jews or Greeks, whether slaves or free—and have all been made to drink into one Spirit" (1 Cor. 12:13).

Nowhere in the Bible are we commanded to be baptized by the Holy Spirit. When we receive Christ as Savior, we are immediately baptized by the Spirit into the Body of Christ. This is a once-for-all, non-recurring experience. When the Holy Spirit came at Pentecost, all who believed were baptized by the Spirit, and, thus, the Body of Christ was formed (Acts 1:4-5). In Acts 2, Jewish believers were baptized by the Spirit. They were, also, filled with the Spirit, empowered to witness and through them multitudes came to Christ.

In Acts 10 Gentile believers had the same experience (Acts 10:44-48; 11:15-17). The baptism by the Holy Spirit accompanied by speaking in tongues first by Jewish believers, then, by Gentile believers revealed that the church was made up of both Jews and Gentiles. Salvation was not only for the Jews but also for the Gentiles. Later, Paul wrote to the church in Rome, " . . . the gospel of Christ . . . is the power of God to salvation for everyone who believes, for the Jew first and also for the Greek" (Rom. 1:16). This initial baptism, in two stages first with Jewish Believers and, then, with Gentile Believers, has never been repeated, and it cannot be any more than Calvary could be repeated. It is, however, made personal for all believers when we trust Christ. The Spirit enters into us and indwells in us. We are baptized into the Body of Christ at that very moment. This means we are a part of the Body of Christ.

The Holy Spirit baptizes every believer into the Body of Christ simultaneously with the new birth. The new believer is immersed or incorporated into union with Jesus. Through the Holy Spirit He is in us and we are in Him. We are one with Him and one with the Father.

The new believer is, also, incorporated spiritually into unity with all other believers in the Body of Christ. We become part of one another and part of the body as whole. We are inter-related with and inter-dependent on one another.

This marvelous reality provides the possibility for all the spiritual gifts to synergistically complement one another and be used in teamship in ministry and witness. The spirit of unity of all the members enhances the power of each individual in witness and ministry. It gives a church body the ability to do all God has for it to do in reaching its area for Christ and in reaching out to the world beyond.

Indwelling of the Holy Spirit—1 Corinthians 6:19-20

At the moment a person receives Christ, the Holy Spirit enters that life to regenerate and create a new spiritual life in Christ. The Holy Spirit never leaves. He permanently indwells the new believer. "Do you not know that your body is the temple of the Holy Spirit who is in you, whom you have from God, and you are not your own? For you were bought at a price; therefore glorify God in your body and spirit which are God's" (1 Cor. 6:19-20).

The church as a corporate body is the temple of the Holy Spirit. The carnal Corinthian church with its superior gifts and its spiritual pride needed to be matured in its understanding of the body-life of the church. It is a Body that is to utilize every spiritual gift in lifting up the Head, the Lord Jesus, and in witnessing and ministering for Him. Instead, they were quarreling over who was greatest and whose spiritual gifts were most important. They needed to remember that the Holy Spirit had indwelt them. They were not their own. The church belonged to Christ! They belonged totally to the One who purchased them with His blood. All the efforts and energy of the church should be given to obey and bring glory to Him.

The Holy Spirit indwells all of us as individual believers! Christ through the Holy Spirit lives in each of us. What a tremendous reality and possibility this is! All Jesus is, He is in us! The Omnipotent Creator with all His mighty power is resident in us. The one who possesses every gift lives within us. Any spiritual gift needed to do anything He wants us to do is available through Him. What tremendous potential! Everywhere we go, Jesus goes—in and through us to do again all He did when He was here in the flesh! Everywhere one of us goes, Jesus is touching people, loving people, ministering to people, bringing people to God through us. He lives in us through the Holy Spirit.

The key is our surrender! We are BOUGHT! We are paid for. We are not our own! Therefore, we must take hands off our own life and yield totally to Christ. Then, we will glorify God in the things we do with our bodies and in our attitudes, emotions, and spirit.

Sealed by the Holy Spirit—Ephesians 1:13-14; 4:30

When we are born again and the Holy Spirit begins to indwell in us, we are also sealed by the Holy Spirit. "In Him you also trusted, after you heard the word of truth, the gospel of your salvation; in whom also, having believed, you were **sealed** with the Holy Spirit of promise, who is the guarantee of our inheritance until the redemption of the purchased possession, to the praise of His glory" (Eph. 1:13-14).

The person who receives Christ is born again, baptized and indwelt by the Holy Spirit. The fourth transaction accomplished is the sealing of the Holy Spirit. What is the significance of this seal of the Spirit?

The Holy Spirit is Himself the seal. This means that the salvation of the believer is absolutely secure because of His work and abiding presence. In four ways this great truth and comforting reality is conveyed.

First, the word seal means "a guarantee or escrow." The Holy Spirit is God's guarantee, escrow, or down payment. The Holy Spirit is the "Spirit of Promise" given to us to guarantee that God will go through with what He said He would do in completing His good work in us and in taking us to heaven. When someone purchases real estate, the person deposits "earnest or escrow money" to guarantee that he or she will go through with the deal. The Holy Spirit is in us as believers. He is God's down payment to assure us that He will never leave us. We cannot be lost again and go to hell.

Second, the seal of the Holy Spirit is like a stamp God puts on our life. When we mail a letter, we purchase a stamp and place it on the envelope. The Postal Services guarantee to get the letter to the destination to which we addressed it. God has guaranteed by giving us the Holy Spirit that He will get us to heaven where He said He would.

Third, the seal of the Holy Spirit is a designation of God's official act of redeeming us and saving us. In biblical times, a king possessed a signet ring. He would press down the signet ring into wax placed on a document to designate it as an official transaction. Because our Lord has paid our sin debt with His sinless blood, the Holy Spirit was given to us when we received Christ. He is the indicator that we have officially become God's children in His family.

Fourth, the word seal carries the idea of a "brand." The seal of the Holy Spirit in our lives is like a brand to designate ownership. Farmers and ranchers brand their animals to designate ownership. The seal or brand shows that the animal belongs to the owner of the brand. By giving us the Holy Spirit, God says, "This one belongs to Me!"

When we are saved, God gives us the Holy Spirit as His seal in our lives. The Spirit communicates God's promise to our hearts. "The Spirit Himself bears witness with our spirit that we are the children of God" (Rom. 8:16). The peace God gives through the seal of the Holy Spirit frees a believer to follow Christ in absolute surrender. Satan has no authority over believers. We have no reason to fear being separated from God. We are eternally secure in Christ. We do not have to labor through the bondage of human works and endless efforts to make sure of our salvation. We are released to walk in the Spirit and to experience His enabling power in every day life. The lives of believers are empowered to produce the fruit of the Spirit. We have the supernatural ability to live lives of peace, love, joy, and patience as well as the other qualities of fruit the spirit gives. As believers, we are equipped to dynamically use the gifts of the Spirit in serving Christ. Our witness becomes effective because of the Holy Spirit within us.

These first four transactions of the Holy Spirit are one-time, non-recurring experiences. A believer is born of the Spirit one time and one time only. It is never repeated. We cannot be "unborn" once we are born into the family of God. As God's children we are "kept by the power of God through faith for salvation" (1 Pet. 1:5). The baptism of the Spirit is forever. It never happens again. The believer is forever "in Christ" and a part of the church of our Lord because of the baptism of the Holy Spirit. The indwelling of the Spirit is once for all. The Holy Spirit never leaves us. The sealing of the Spirit is permanent. If it were not, it would not be a guarantee. It is based on God's unshakable promise to guide, grow, and keep His child. God's promise is that He will get us to heaven and complete His good work of making us like Jesus.

Filled With the Holy Spirit – Ephesians 5:18; Acts 4:31

The fifth transaction of the Holy Spirit at conversion is the "filling of the Spirit." While the first four are non-recurring experiences, the filling of the Holy Spirit does happen again and again. The baptism of the Spirit only happens once in our lives, but we need fresh fillings repeatedly as the Apostles experienced in the book of Acts. The power of the Holy Spirit is necessary for living in victory, preaching and witnessing. The apostles were filled with the Spirit in Acts 2 at Pentecost; then, they experienced repeated fillings after that (Acts 4:8, 31; 6:3, 5; 7:55; 13:9).

"And do not be drunk with wine, in which is dissipation; but be filled with the Spirit" (Eph. 5:18). The word "be filled" means to be *controlled by* or *under the influence of* the Holy Spirit. It has nothing to do with a quantity needed to fill an empty container. It is not as though we are empty vessels that must have a certain quantity of fuel to keep us going. Instead, we are God's creation by our natural birth and God's children by our spiritual birth. We are indwelt by the Holy Spirit, but we are also to be controlled by the Spirit. We are not to be satisfied simply to have Him present in our lives, but He wants to be preeminent. He is not to be just a passenger, but He is pilot of the ship of our lives.

This is why the negative "be not drunk with wine" is given as the first half of the verse. When people are drunk (filled with) wine, they are under its control or influence. In Luke 4:28 "They , , , were filled with wrath" means "they were controlled or were under the influence of wrath" and they tried to kill Jesus. We are to be controlled by the Spirit who lives in us.

"Be filled" is in the imperative mood, a command. The verb is very interesting and packed with meaning. The verb is in the imperative mood, which places it in the realm of a command or strong exhortation. We have no choice in the matter. There is no excuse that validates our failure to be filled with the Spirit. We are commanded by an omniscient, omnipotent God to do so; therefore, we can do it! God would never command us to do anything that is impossible for us. He would never command us to do a thing without equipping and enabling us to do it.

None of us is excluded! From the least to the best-known believer, from the most recent convert to the one who has been a follower of Christ for a half a century, we are all included as God gives the command. The verb is plural in its number. This means it covers every believer. At times we like to rationalize that our circumstances are too difficult or people have mistreated us, so therefore it is understandable that we are not filled. But, there really are no reasons not to allow the Holy Spirit to control our lives. Our low points are when we need His control, guidance, and power more than ever. We must be controlled by the Holy Spirit or live in disobedience and settle for less than God's best for us.

The verb, "be filled," is in the passive voice, which means that the subject is acted upon. Being filled with or controlled by the Spirit is not something we do to or for ourselves. God does it! It is not something we accomplish by our own effort, earn by our good works, or purchase by our giving money or time. It is the act of God in our lives in response to our surrender to Him. When we are humbly broken before Him, confess and turn from our sin, experience His cleansing, and yield to the control of His Lordship, the Spirit takes control of our lives. We are filled with His Spirit

We go on in His fullness, and under His control until we sin again. Then, we are no longer filled with and controlled by the Spirit. But, here is an exciting aspect of this single verb. The verb is in the present tense. Present tense in the Greek language denotes continuous (on-going) action! It is saying, "Continue to keep on allowing the Holy Spirit to have control of you!"

When we, like the apostles, take our eyes off Jesus and we allow fear or other pressures to distract us from Him and His mission for us, we can stop, look at ourselves honestly, confess our sin, and be filled anew with the Spirit. It is an on-going process! It is a moment-by-moment experience of trusting and yielding to Him. Our past is not a prelude to our future! Just because we fouled up doesn't mean we have to continue to live in defeat. God wants us to turn to Him the moment we realize we are out of fellowship with Him and no longer controlled by the Spirit. He wants to forgive, cleanse, fill us, and restore us.

Dr. Bill Bright, president of Campus Crusade for Christ, has illustrated this spiritual principle by comparing it to physical breathing. He teaches us how to practice spiritual breathing. We live physically by breathing—that is, we exhale and expel the stale air from our lungs. We inhale by receiving fresh air to energize us. We, also, live in victory by breathing spiritually—that is, we exhale by confessing our sins that stifle and defeat us. We inhale by receiving by faith the fullness of the Holy Spirit and yielding to His control. Then, we walk in the Spirit and victory occurs!

Our focus must be on the Giver of spiritual gifts, not on the gifts themselves. The Giver is the Triune God—Father, Son and Holy Spirit. God, the Father, so loved the world that He gave His only begotten Son, Jesus Christ, that we might be born of the Holy Spirit. God, the Holy Spirit, who lives within us gives gifts to us as believers to enable us to glorify the Son and carry out His mission in this earth.

The Holy Spirit is our salvation gift! He is the "power formula" for our individual lives as believers and for the Body of Christ corporately. He sovereignty surfaces spiritual gifts and distributes them in the Body as He sees best according to our personalities, needs, and calling. He omnisciently superintends their utilization for effectiveness. He omnipotently empowers their utilization to accomplish His glorious purpose.

ACTIVITIES

Why do you think this chapter is named "God's Power Formula"?

_____

_____

_____

What are the four, one-time, permanent transactions of the Holy Spirit at the time of conversion?

1. _____
2. _____
3. _____
4. _____

Are you filled with the Spirit? ____ yes ____ no Do you want to be? ____ yes ____ no If you checked "yes" to both answers, then practice 1 John 1:9 by doing the following:

1. Take a sheet of paper. Pray and ask the Holy Spirit to show you yourself. Write down on the paper every sin and shortcoming of your life.

2. Name your sins to God. Confess them as sin. Ask God to forgive you. Tear up and throw away the paper or burn it. Realize God has put your sins as far from you as the east is from the west. He remembers them no more.

3. Ask the Holy Spirit to fill you and take control of your life.

4. Claim His fullness.

5. Act in obedience to Christ, and go on to live for Him.

Chapter Three

Spotlight on Gifts
Outline

When the Scriptures deal with gifts, they do so in the context of instructions about the Body of Christ.

I. Spiritual Gifts Are Sovereign Grace Endowments Given to Believers
- What Is a Spiritual Gift?
- When Are Spiritual Gifts Given?

II. Spiritual Gifts are Distributed by the Holy Spirit
- The Holy Spirit Mediates and Arranges Gifts in the Body
- The Holy Spirit Empowers. Gifts When Believers Obey

III. Spiritual Gifts are Given through Individual Believers
- Ministry Is Effective as Individual Members Use Them to Build Up the Body
- Maturity Is Not Guaranteed Because One Is Exceptionally Gifted
- Maturity Is Mandatory for Maximum Effectiveness

IV. Spiritual Gifts Belong to the Body for Its Edification
- Members are Responsible to the Body
- The Body Is Responsible to Christ for Its Ministry
  Enlighten Believers about Gifts
  Enlist Believers to Use Their Gifts
  Involve Members in Utilizing Their Gifts

46

V. Spiritual Gifts May Be Counterfeited by Satan
- Deception of the Counterfeit
- Deception about Gifts—Counterfeit Gifts
- Deception about Leaders
- Detection of the Counterfeit
  Apply the Scripture Test
  Apply the Moral Test
  Apply the Evangelistic Test

Chapter Three

Spotlight on Gifts

The major biblical passages about spiritual gifts are found in the context of Bible verses about the church, the Body of Christ. The Body of Christ belongs to our Lord. Every believer is a part of the general Body and is to be member of a local body of believers. We, as individual believers, belong to our Lord! We belong to Him, first, by creation and, second, by re-creation. By our first birth we become a part of the human family created by the Almighty God. But, by our second birth—spiritual regeneration through Christ—we became part of the family of God. God desires that every member of the human family become a member of His family (1 Tim. 2:4).

God's plan for humanity is revealed in His Word, the Bible. It reveals His plan of redemption through which He reaches out to the human family and offers to bring those who respond to His love and forgiveness through Christ into His spiritual family.

The Bible is God's manual for successful living. It is the creator's guide to show us how to live with fullness and fruitfulness. It is in the Bible, the Word of God, that we find our instruction about spiritual gifts. The Bible gives us, as His children, what we need to know about His pronouncements, promises, and principles relating to spiritual gifts.

Five truths are given or implied in the Bible that help us understand the relationship of spiritual gifts to the Body of Christ.

1. Spiritual gifts are sovereign grace endowments to Believers.
   Rom. 12:6; 1 Cor. 12:11; Jer. 1:5
2. Spiritual gifts are distributed by the Holy Spirit.
   1 Cor. 12:11
3. Spiritual gifts are given through individual believers.

1 Cor. 12:11; 1 Cor. 14:12
4. Spiritual gifts belong to the Body, the church.
1 Cor. 14:12
5. Spiritual gifts are sometimes counterfeited by Satan.
2 Cor. 11;13-15

1. Spiritual Gifts are Sovereign Grace Endowments by God to Believers

Our sovereign God has graciously chosen to supernaturally endow each of us as a believer with spiritual gifts to enable us to be a meaningful member of the Body of Christ and to effectively serve Him. But, what is a *spiritual gift*? Many variations of definitions have been given.

In his book, *Systematic Theology; An Introduction to Biblical Doctrine,* Dr. Wayne Grudem says, "A spiritual gift is any ability that is empowered by the Holy Spirit and used in any ministry of the church." Dr. Grudem chose this broad definition to include both gifts that are related to natural abilities and those that seem to be more miraculous.

Regardless of theological definitions, it is apparent as you study Scripture that a spiritual gift is a special ability that our sovereign God, by His grace, has placed within the life of a believer for building up the church, the Body of Christ. Through no merit of our own, our omniscient, omnipotent Creator has chosen to give us supernaturally empowered abilities. Paul reminded young Timothy to " . . . stir up the gift of God which is in you" (2 Tim. 1:6).

When God called Jeremiah, He spoke to him about his giftedness, "Before I formed you in the womb I knew you; before you were born I sanctified you; I ordained you to be a prophet to the nations" (Jer. 1:5).

Jeremiah answered the Lord, "Behold I cannot speak, for I am a youth" (v. 6). "But the Lord said to me: 'Do not say, I am a youth,' For you shall go to all to whom I send you. And whatever I command you, you shall speak. Do not be afraid of their faces, for I am with you to deliver you,' says the Lord" (vv. 7-8) James 1:17 says, "Every good gift and every perfect gift is from above, and comes down from the Father of lights, with whom there is no variation or shadow of turning."

What He expects us to do, He equips us to do! He gave Timothy gifts for the pastoral and evangelistic ministry to which He called him. From the context of Paul's letters to Timothy, we conclude that Timothy was somewhat shy and introverted. The gifts of God to accomplish God's will and work were within him. If he would take the initiative to do what God called him to do, the gifts to do it would surface. Paul encouraged him, "Do not neglect the gift that is in you" (1 Tim. 4:14). The reality is that we can neglect the gifts within us. Like Timothy we need to "stir up the gift within us."

Jeremiah was called to the difficult ministry of "tearing down and building up." Such a ministry seemed impossible. But, God not only had given Jeremiah the temperament for such a confrontive, prophetic ministry, He, also, gave His sorrowful and shy servant the ability to speak when he did not think he could.

When God called me, the Spirit of God impressed on my mind and heart that I should preach the gospel of Christ. At the time I was 17 years old. In spite of His call, I knew I could not do it! It was out of the realm of possibility! But, His heavy hand remained on my life until I could stand it no longer. During the Sunday-morning worship service, I surrendered my life and will to Him and made a public commitment to preach. The next morning as I was about to leave for high school, Roy Fish stopped by my home. Roy was a seminary student-pastor from a nearby church. He had heard about my recent decision.

Pastor Fish took my hand and said, "Darrell, I understand you surrendered to preach yesterday."

"Yes, I did, Pastor Fish," I said.

"I am going to be gone from my church a week from Sunday. Will you preach for me?"

What a shock! I had no idea what I would say. I did not know what a sermon was. I could not even lead in public prayer! I did not even own a Bible! I borrowed my mother's old tattered Bible to preach from for the first few months of my ministry. I did not have a suit to wear. I wore cowboy boots and Levis. I thought a preacher had to wear a suit, so I went to town and bought a suit!

Nevertheless, I had settled that issue. God had called me to preach, and I had surrendered my life. I said, "Yes, Brother Fish, I will do it."

I did not know where to start! I had no idea what I would do. I never intended to be a preacher. My great ambition growing up in West Texas on a cotton-and-cattle farm was to go to Texas A & M University and get a degree in veterinary medicine. I wanted to make enough money to buy a cattle ranch and enjoy life. I loved the animals. You don't have to talk to them, and I was not a talker. My wife asks, "What happened to you?" Now, I talk all the time!

But, God knew me better than I knew myself! He knew how and why He made me. He knew the gifts that were within me! He had given them to me, and He wanted to use me for His plan.

I went to see my pastor for help. He taught me a little about sermon structure. He told me sermons must have points. I wondered about that, because I have heard a lot of sermons that I wondered if they had a point! And, I have preached some like that!

I bought a little New Testament and took it with me as I drove the tractor planting cotton. I held it on the tractor steering wheel and read while I drove. We had the crookedest rows in the country that year. I frantically read through the book of Romans, where I found a text that spoke to me: Romans 8:—"There is therefore now no condemnation to those who are in Christ Jesus, who do not walk according to the flesh, but according to the Spirit." I began to get points for my sermon and finally got eight. None of them had anything to do with the text, but I had a text and eight points!

Every evening I would practice my sermon in our garage. I used mother's old washing machine for my pulpit, and the deep freeze was my congregation. And, I have preached to a lot of church folks just that cold since then! I practiced the sermon about 20 times until I could preach at least 22 minutes. The Sunday came when I was to preach. The house was full of people who had come to hear the "boy preacher."

When I got up to preach, I held on to the pulpit. It shook as much as I did, and I preached every bit of my eight-point, 22-minute sermon in 13 minutes! But when I finished, several people came forward to make decisions for Christ. I had learned something special! Whatever you place in the hands of God is sufficient! He will use whatever you yield to Him! I was nothing but ignorance-on-fire, but God began to use me and continued to do so. Pastors began to invite me to preach for them, and God continued to bless. Since that time, I have preached almost every week. Through His grace, God had sovereignly given me gifts necessary to do what He planned for me to do.

Without question, I had the option of saying, "Yes!" or "No!" to what God impressed on my life. I faced the choice of neglecting the gifts He had given me or using and developing them.

When Are Spiritual Gifts Given?

Our spiritual gifts are sovereign endowments given by God by grace. But an interesting question is, "When does God give His gifts to us?"

At least three possible answers exist:

Some say, "He gives them to us when we receive Christ and are born of the Spirit." That is when the Holy Spirit distributes to us gifts to use in building up the Body.

Others say, "The Holy Spirit distributes spiritual gifts to us when the need arises." If this is true, gifts would come suddenly as the need to use them arises.

I would propose a third alternative—that at the time of conception when our total personality and being are being formed, God gives us our temperament and intelligence and places within us the potential gifts for our service to Him.

Certainly, merit exists for any one of these three answers.

First, the Holy Spirit transacts the new birth and indwells our lives when we receive Christ. His power is present within us, and we begin to serve our Lord. He is the one who distributes gifts through the Body of Christ. He empowers us to use them. It can appear, then, that we receive spiritual gifts when we experience salvation.

Second, when the need arises for using a gift, it becomes apparent that the gift is present in our lives. It can appear that spiritual gifts are given as the need and opportunity for exercising them arises. This was the case in my life. I had no realization of my giftedness until I began to obey what God was leading me to do. When I yielded my life to obey His will, God gave me the ability to do it. It was marvelous to me to see what God was doing as the Holy Spirit surfaced the gifts needed for me to preach, pastor and evangelize.

Third, evidence exists that the potential for all we can become is God's gift to us at the time of our conception through His sovereign creative activity. This means that the gift potential is present in our lives to be used however God wants to use us, if we will obey Christ. As I look back over my life, I realize this was true with me. Many of my activities indicated that these gifts were present, but they were not empowered by the Spirit as spiritual gifts.

The Bible does not identify the specific time or occasion when believers are given spiritual gifts. It seems that all three of the possible answers listed above are involved in the full answer to the question. At conception, God stamps into our DNA the potential for personality, intelligence, traits, qualities, abilities, and gifts.

This was true with God's calling and gifting of Jeremiah, the Old Testament prophet. "Then the word of the Lord came to me, saying: 'before I formed you in the womb I knew you; Before you were born I sanctified you; I ordained you a prophet to the nations.' Then said I: 'Ah, Lord God! Behold I cannot speak, for I am a youth.' But the Lord said to me: 'Do not say, 'I am a youth,' For you shall go to all to whom I send you, and whatever I command you, you shall speak" (Jer. 1:4-7).

Through scientific studies of genetics, we see visible evidence supporting what God said to Jeremiah thousands of years ago. At conception, Jeremiah had all the gifts and qualities he would need to obey God and accomplish His purpose for his life. In obeying God and following His plan, Jeremiah's life would have fulfillment. While God does seem to endow us with gifts at conception, we are not empowered to use them as spiritual gifts until we are born spiritually by faith through the work of the Holy Spirit. Then, our gifts are spiritually empowered for kingdom service. The fact that we possess these latent gifts is not apparent until the need to use them arises. Then, the Holy Spirit surfaces them and empowers us to use them as we obey Him. If we resist and do not obey Him, the gift may never surface and never be observed. Paul urged Timothy, "Do not neglect the gift that is in you" (1 Tim. 4:14). Again, he admonished Timothy to "stir up the gift which is within you" (2 Tim. 1:6).

Paul himself is an illustration of this truth. Before he was converted, he used the same gifts to persecute the church and oppose Christ that he used after his conversion to lift up Jesus, spread the gospel, and start churches. The difference is that after conversion, his gifts were surrendered to the Lordship of Christ, the Head of the Body, anointed and empowered by the Holy Spirit and arranged in the

Body "as it pleased Him." Paul shares this testimony in Galatians 1:11-24. He says in verses 15 and 16, "But when it pleased God, who separated me from my mother's womb and called me through His grace, to reveal His Son in me, that I might preach Him among the Gentiles." Paul was gifted by the Almighty, Sovereign, Beneficent God at his conception. Through His grace, God overshadowed Paul until he was converted and, then, empowered him to use his gifts in the work of the Kingdom. As Saul of Tarsus, he was a highly gifted, intensely focused person. He used the gifts God had given him against Christ and His church. When he received Christ, these same gifts were transformed into gifts that the Holy Spirit anointed. They were powerfully used for the worldwide expansion of Christianity.

Even non-believers have God-given gifts latent within them. But their gifts will never be activated through Holy Spirit's power until they receive Christ as Savior and Lord and seek to obey Him.

Is there a distinction between "human talents" and gifts? I find no biblical evidence for such a distinction. They are one and the same. Our beneficent Creator is the giver of both (Jas. 1:17.) Call them whatever we will, non-believers use God-given abilities, talents, or "gifts" very successfully and sometimes for great achievements. However, their gifts are not Holy-Spirit empowered and directed until the person receives Christ. When non-believers are converted, the Holy Spirit indwells them and surfaces gifts that they begin to use in obedience to Him. It is then that they become "spiritual gifts." What tremendous potential God has given us if we will only yield to Him and allow Him to use the gifts He has given us.

Albert Einstein, for example, was another highly gifted person. He used his gifts for the benefit of humanity. What tremendous potential he had for service to Christ, but he never received our Lord. His gifts never became spiritual gifts and were never anointed by the Spirit to build up the Body of Christ.

Adolf Hitler also had exceptional gifts. He had a charismatic personality with an ability to persuade, organize, and lead. But, he prostituted and perverted God's gifts for evil. The atrocities he committed were a result of his choices to reject Christ and follow Satan's path of pride and self-ambition.

Spiritual gifts are given to us from our perfect, loving, omniscient Father. He knows how to give good gifts to His children (Luke

11:13). He has committed to give us His highest and best. He has not withheld from us His very best gift, His own Son! (Rom. 8:32)

Spiritual Gifts Are Distributed by the Holy Spirit

God gives spiritual gifts to individuals through the work of the Holy Spirit. At conception, the Holy Spirit stamps the potential of our gifts into our DNA. When we receive Christ, they are transformed into spiritual gifts. At the appropriate time of need He surfaces them to be used. He is sovereign in distributing spiritual gifts to members throughout the Body. "But one and the same Spirit works all these things, distributing to each one individually as He wills" (1 Cor. 12:11). "There are diversities of gifts, but the same Spirit. There are differences of ministries, but the same Lord" (1 Cor. 12:4-5). Like a human body which has numerous organs that function effectively, no useless organs exist in the Body of Christ. Each has some function.

The Holy Spirit mediates and arranges gifts in the Body to complement each other. A musician cannot produce harmonious melody from a single note, nor an artist a masterpiece with one color. Similarly the Spirit's purpose can only be accomplished by means of several gifts. He leads individual members in how to use his or her gifts. He interprets the will of God to hearts and minds for their ministries in the Body of Christ. Through His filling of individual lives, He empowers believers to use their gifts to accomplish outstanding achievements for the glory of Christ and the good of the Body.

Obedience to the Holy Spirit is the key to the effectiveness of the individual believer and the corporate Body of Christ. When we live our daily lives filled with and under the control of the Holy Spirit, He has the liberty to lead, place, and use our gifts where they can accomplish the most. *The Body functions best when we work in teamship so that gifts enhance one another and ministries complement each other.* Self-centeredness and pride will cause us to draw away from other members to attempt to use our gifts in isolation from the rest of the Body. It is often easier to simply focus on our own gift and use it in isolation because to minister in teamship requires us to consider others. It means we have to practice the fruit of the Spirit such as love and patience rather than simply having only ourselves to consider. We have to grow meaningful relationships where we encourage and support others. We have to learn to place others ahead of ourselves and often allow them to serve even when we think we might do better. We will be glad to give praise and credit to others instead of performing for accolades for ourselves. It is in the context of the Body-life of the church that God grows us into the image of Christ.

Spiritual Gifts Are Given through Individual Believers

Spiritual gifts are personal. Machines, instruments, and organizations cannot possess spiritual gifts. They are given to individual members. The powerful potential of the church resides in the spiritual gifts in the lives of believers. It is God's will for each member of the Body to do the work of ministry. "And He Himself gave some (gifts) to be apostles, some prophets, some evangelists, and some pastors and teachers, for the equipping of the saints for the work of the ministry, for the edifying of the body of Christ" (Eph. 4:11-12). Therefore, God enables every believer to serve by giving him or her spiritual gifts for ministry. "As each one has received a gift, minister it to one another, as good stewards of the manifold grace of God" (1 Pet. 4:10).

Gifts Do Not Guarantee Spiritual Maturity

Even immature Christians have spiritual gifts and can use them. This was evident in the Corinthian church, which had an abundance of spiritual gifts (1 Cor. 1:7). Yet, it was still very immature in many areas of doctrine and conduct. Paul says, "And I, brethren, could not speak to you as spiritual people but as to carnal, as to babes in Christ" (1 Cor. 3:1). Spiritual gifts, then, are not a sign of spiritual maturity. It is possible to have remarkable spiritual gifts in one area or another but to be very spiritually immature in spiritual understanding and in Christian conduct.

On some occasions even unbelievers are able to prophesy and cast out demons and do miracles. Jesus says, "Not everyone who says to Me, 'Lord, Lord,' shall enter the kingdom of heaven, but he who does the will of My Father in heaven. Many will say to Me in that day, 'Lord, Lord,' have we not prophesied in Your name, cast out demons in Your name, and done many wonders in Your name? And then I will declare to them, 'I never knew you; depart from Me, you who practice lawlessness!" (Matt. 7:21-23) They had done mighty works, but they were never Christians. So we cannot evaluate spiritual maturity on the basis of spiritual gifts.

Maturity comes through walking with Christ in the fullness of the Spirit. "He who says he abides in Him ought himself also to walk just as He walked" (1 John 2:6). The Holy Spirit produces the "fruit of the Spirit" in the life of the mature believer. "I say then: Walk in the Spirit, and you shall not fulfill the lust of the flesh . . . But the fruit of the Spirit is love, joy, peace, longsuffering, kindness, goodness, faithfulness, gentleness, self-control. Against such there is no law. And those who are Christ's have crucified the flesh with its passions and desires. If we live in the Spirit, let us also walk in the Spirit" (Gal. 5:16, 22-25). Christ-likeness in character, speech, and behavior is the mark of spiritual maturity. A person may have outstanding gifts without Christ-likeness. But, what tremendous power for ministry exists in a life that demonstrates the fruit of the Spirit and uses spiritual gifts in a Christ-like way!

God's great purpose for every believer is to develop in Christlikeness. As Christians, we are in the process of growth so that Christ is being formed in us. The Holy Spirit is constantly at work within us so we will become all we can be in Christ. In this life we are developing the character we will have through all eternity. Gifts cannot make us Christ-like! But <u>Christlikeness immeasurably enhances the effectiveness of spiritual gifts</u>. "But also for this very reason, giving all diligence, add to your faith virtue, to virtue knowledge, to knowledge self-control, to self-control perseverance, to perseverance godliness, to godliness brotherly kindness, and to brotherly kindness love. For if these things are yours and abound, you will be neither barren nor unfruitful in the knowledge of our Lord Jesus Christ" (2 Pet. 1:5-8).

Spiritual gifts enable the believer to be useful in the service and witness of Christ. The Body becomes effective as the Holy Spirit distributes gifts through the individual members.

Spiritual Gifts Belong to the Body for Its Edification

The Body of Christ is the custodian of spiritual gifts. These gifts are given to the Body through individual members for the work of ministry, but they belong to the church for its edification. Paul instructs the Corinthian Christians to regulate the use of their gifts for the building up of the church. "So it is with you, Since you are eager to have spiritual gifts, try to excel in gifts that build up the church" (1 Cor. 14:12 NIV). The entire passage of 1 Corinthians 14 is Paul's outline of procedures for the church to follow in making sure that gifts are used in an orderly way that will exalt the Lord, edify the church, encourage other believers, and evangelize the lost.

In Ephesians 4:11-12 apostles, prophets, evangelists, pastors, and teachers are told to utilize their gifts "for the equipping of the saints for the work of ministry, for the edifying of the body of Christ."

In 1 Corinthians 12 individual members are told in verse 7 that each gift is "for the profit of all"; in verse 11 that He "distributes to each one individually"; in verse 14 that "the body is not one member but many"; in verse 25 that "there should be no schism in the body," and that "members should have the same care for one another."

All of these instructions and admonitions indicate that individual members are to be subject to the Body of Christ over which He is the Head. "And He is the head of the body, the church, who is the beginning, the firstborn from the dead, that in all things He may have the preeminence" (Col. 1:18). We are to use our particular spiritual gifts to exalt the Savior, to edify the Body, to equip the people of God, and to evangelize non-believers. As individual members, we must realize that our gifts are not for our own self-aggrandizement, nor for our use to gain position, nor for our profiteering. The gifts belong to the Body. We are to surrender our gifts to the Body of Christ and to use them within the Body.

At one time I wrote some material that was helpful in seeing our church reach non-believers and experience significant growth. I taught the material in a conference. Some of the conference participants asked, "May we use this material in our church? We would like to modify it and apply it to the needs of our situation."

I was glad to be able to say, "This material is not my own. God gave it to me through the Holy Spirit. It belongs to the Body of Christ for its edification. Use it however the Holy Spirit directs you."

What Is the Church to Do About Spiritual Gifts of Its Members?

Not only do the individual members have a responsibility to the Body of Christ for the use of their gifts, but the Body has a responsibility to Christ for its members. What is the responsibility of the Body? A church should do four things regarding its responsibility:

First, the church should <u>enlighten</u> members. Many members know nothing about spiritual gifts and have no idea that they have them. Many church members are living in spiritual defeat. They do not think there is anything they can do for their Lord. Their spiritual self-esteem is at rock bottom. Pastors and leaders need to enlighten members about spiritual gifts. People need to be taught what the Word of God has to say about their gifts. When they realize that God has gifted them for the "work of ministry" (Eph. 4:11-12), church members will be motivated and greatly encouraged.

Second, the church should <u>enlist</u> believers for places of service in witness and ministry. Spiritual gifts begin to surface in the lives of believers when they start to obey Christ in witnessing to people and in ministering to those who have need. Most will not begin to use their gifts until they are affirmed and enlisted by their church. It is important for churches to develop broad enough action plans and ministries to be able to involve every member. This means that the strategy of the church *must not be programmatic*. It cannot set up enough programmatic positions to involve every member. Instead, it must focus on the strategic plan of Jesus for witness and ministry. Every member can witness and minister to people. In doing so they can begin to exercise their various gifts.

Third, for maximum involvement of members, churches must <u>equip</u> their people to use their gifts effectively. Our gracious God gives gifts to believers, but these must be developed through training and equipping to be most effective. This can be done through individual as well as group training. Classes and seminars are necessary. Members can be involved in on-the-job training. The entire church needs to be equipped through the pulpit preaching of the pastor and special guest speakers. Regardless of methodology, believers must be equipped to use their gifts.

Fourth, the church needs to build processes to *<u>involve</u>* members in utilizing their gifts. To involve every member means that the church will set up multiple types of ministries to touch and help people. The need for such ministries exists in every community. What is required is for the church to be sensitive to the people in its area. The church will, also, need to set up multiple types of witness and outreach activities at various times to be able to involve the most members in reaching people. It will need to emphasize marketplace and lifestyle witnessing for believers to share Christ where they live, work and play every day.

A healthy church is one filled with joyful members who have realized that God has given them gifts for ministry and they are faithfully using their gifts to glorify Him. There is nothing more powerful than a church filled with believers who are living in unity, in joyful fellowship with one another, and in obedience to Christ.

Spiritual Gifts May Be Counterfeited by Satan

Our Lord wants to use every member and that person's spiritual gifts to build up His Body. But, our Lord Jesus Christ is not the only one who has a purpose for your spiritual gifts. *Satan, also, makes his bid to use our spiritual gifts in his service.* He will attempt to use any emphasis on spiritual gifts and any individual to confuse believers and create conflict in the church.

Satan is the master tempter and deceiver. Any time the church is filled with the fire of God's presence and Christians are obediently using their gifts to reach the lost, disciple converts, and minister to people, Satan will not be pleased. He will attempt to disrupt the good work the Holy Spirit is doing.

Satan has no better tool than disunity and internal conflict. He will try to disrupt and defeat what God is doing by counterfeiting the gifts of the Spirit. He will send people into the church who are attractive and have latent God-given gifts, but they are under Satan's control. They pervert the goodness and gifts of God that are in them. They are filled with pride and self-seeking. They seek to gain influence, establish themselves in control positions, and divert the church from the direction of the Holy Spirit. They create confusion, disrupt the fellowship, and render it powerless.

Satan is the ultimate deceiver. Paul writes, "For such are false apostles, deceitful workers, transforming themselves into apostles of Christ. And no wonder! For Satan himself transforms himself into an angel of light. Therefore it is no great thing if his ministers also transform themselves into ministers of righteousness, whose end will be according to their works" (2 Cor. 11:13-15).

Acts 5 says when the church was filled with power and multitudes were being saved, the believers were in one accord and were giving with abandon to meet the needs of people who were being reached. Barnabas sold property and gave all the money into the church treasury. Evidently he was highly regarded for his unselfish sharing. Pride filled the hearts of two members, Ananias and Sapphira. They desired the same kind of recognition. So, they sold property and conspired to feign giving it all while they instead kept back a portion for themselves. Thus, Satan's strategy was to send in his representatives as hypocrites to dilute the powerful, Christ-centered fellowship to render it impotent. Their hypocrisy was easily detectable in such a genuine fellowship. The Apostle Peter stood and confronted it. The Holy Spirit smote them. They both died on the spot! They had attempted to counterfeit the gift of giving in the early church. Barnabas had the genuine gift of giving. Ananias and Sapphira were counterfeiters! It is dangerous to be the instrument of Satan to attempt to disrupt a Christ-centered, Holy Spirit directed church. God will deal severely with them!

Paul warned the church at Ephesus, "For I know this, that after my departure savage wolves will come in among you, not sparing the flock. Also from among yourselves men will rise up, speaking perverse things, to draw away the disciples after themselves" (Acts 20:29-30). These would be counterfeit pastors, teachers, prophets, evangelists, etc.

At times Satan will use the self-centered, false professors of Christ to counterfeit the works of God and gain them as his followers. By this means he infiltrates the church to create confusion and chaos. At other times he will attack genuine believers who are legitimately using their gifts to edify the church. He will tempt them with pride that produces an attitude of self-centeredness and competition among believers. The unity of the church is destroyed as Christ is no longer its focus. It loses its passion for the lost and forsakes its mission to reach them for Christ. This is what apparently happened in the church of Corinth through their intense interest in spiritual gifts (1 Cor. 12-14).

Satan motivates greedy, self-seeking people to draw away followers after themselves. These people will be highly gifted and very attractive, but insincere. "For many walk, of whom I have told you often, and now tell you even weeping, that they are the enemies of the cross of Christ: whose end is destruction, whose god is their belly, and whose glory is in their shame—who set their mind on earthly things" (Phil. 3:18-19).

Today as in New Testament times false prophets, pastors, evangelists, teachers, leaders, and church members infiltrate the church to gain a following for their own purposes instead of the glory of Christ (Acts 20:29-30). Their objectives are to gain money for themselves, to secure position and recognition, to occupy a place of power and prestige, and to receive personal glory. Jesus spoke about these in Matthew 7:22-23, when He said, "Many will say to Me in that day, 'Lord, Lord, have we not prophesied in Your name, cast out demons in Your name, and done many wonders in Your name?' And then I will declare to them, 'I never knew you; depart from Me, you who practice lawlessness!'"

How to Detect Counterfeit Gifts

Jesus told His apostles a parable about the wheat and tares. He illustrated the truth that counterfeit followers with counterfeit gifts would always be present with the true believers who serve with sincerity. They are difficult to detect. This being true, the question is, "What can we do to keep the fellowship of our churches and the work of our Lord from being decimated by false teachers and leaders?"

TRY THE SPIRITS! Yes, there is something we can do! There are tests that can be applied to any spiritual experience or service to help determine its genuineness. John instructs us to take precautions. He says, "Beloved, do not believe every spirit, but test the spirits, whether they are of God; because many false prophets have gone out into the world. By this you know the Spirit of God: Every spirit that confesses that Jesus Christ has come in the flesh is of God, and every spirit that does not confess that Jesus Christ has come in the flesh is not of God" (1 John 4:1-2).

Three Tests for Gifts

First, the **Scripture test.** Ask the hard question, "Does this "spiritual gift" and the way it is being exercised harmonize with biblical teachings? Does it violate any biblical truth or principle? If it does, then it would not be legitimate. Does it do what the Bible teaches a spiritual gift is to do? Does it exalt the Savior, glorify Him, and edify the church? When people call attention to themselves in their experience or service, it is not of God. We are to glorify Jesus! When the focus is on money and how much can be gained financially by a particular activity or ministry, it is evidence against genuineness of the gift and its use.

Second, the **moral test.** Ask the integrity question, "Does this 'spiritual gift' demonstrate moral purity in its practice, in motivation, and in relationships with others?" If it is of God, it will pass the moral test. The works of the flesh such as lying, financial dishonesty, anger and bitterness, sexual immorality, gossip, and tale-bearing negate the use of spiritual gifts in a person's life.

Third, the **evangelistic test.** Ask the results question, "Does the use of this gift lift up Jesus so that others are drawn to Him? Does its use result in reaching the lost for Christ?" Does it edify the Body of Christ? Any genuine spiritual gift will build up the Body and make it more effective in carrying out His mission to "seek and to save that which is lost."

Counteracting the Counterfeit

The best antidote for counterfeit spirituality is truth. As long as we believe a lie and act on the basis of erroneous information, we will act wrongly. The best antidote for counterfeit spirituality is truth. Jesus said, "You shall know the truth, and the truth shall make you free" (John 8:32). Teach and preach the truth of the Scriptures! In the wilderness temptations of Jesus, our Lord answered Satan's temptations with the Word of God, and Satan was defeated. When believers are grounded in the Word of God, they will be equipped to discern and reject that which is false. They will not reject the "sound mind principle" of Spirit-controlled reasoning and, thus, be carried away by extreme emotion. Neither will they reject God-given emotion and develop a strictly cerebral religious life. They will develop the balance of Holy Spirit directed emotion and reason.

Another defense against the counterfeit in spiritual living and serving is God's warning. Paul warned the young churches he planted against false teachers and ego-driven leaders. He admonished the pastors "to take heed to yourselves and to all the flock, among which the Holy Spirit has made you overseers " (Acts 20:28). Jesus said that the "good shepherd gives His life for the sheep", but a hireling flees when the wolf comes because "he is a hireling and does not care about the sheep" (John 10:11-13). True spiritual leaders must be ready to confront those who would infiltrate the church and bring harm to it as Peter did in the case of Ananias and Sapphira in Acts 5. This requires courage on the part of leaders and a willingness on the part of the church to follow godly pastoral leadership.

Still another essential in defending a church against spiritual counterfeiters is willingness to follow the leadership of the Holy Spirit. Again, obedience is the key! The Holy Spirit leads and fills His own. He bears witness with our spirits that we are the children of God. He brings a unity between those who are His. When the unity is being threatened, we need to stop and seek His leadership to act positively in removing the factor creating disunity.

God's sovereignty endows believers with spiritual gifts that are distributed by the Holy Spirit through individuals to the church, the Body of Christ! Gifts belong to the Body for its edification to enable it *to exalt the Savior, equip the saints, and evangelize the sinner.*

ACTIVITIES

Discuss the following questions in your study group or answer them yourself:

1. When did Jeremiah receive his gift to be a prophet?

_____

_____

_____

2. What is a spiritual gift?

_____

_____

_____

3. What is the relationship between spiritual gifts and spiritual maturity in the life of a believer?

_____

_____

_____

4. What is the overshadowing purpose of spiritual gifts?

_____

_____

_____

5. What are the tests for helping you discern counterfeit gifts?

_____

_____

_____

Chapter Four

Getting a Grip on Your Gifts

Outline

It is important that we know what to do with our spiritual gifts. The following are five principles for using spiritual gifts:

I. Spiritual Gifts Are to Be Used, Not Left Dormant
 • Keep Your Mind Renewed through Submission to God
 • Trust God with Your Life
 • Yield to God and Be Willing to Do His Will
II. Spiritual Gifts Are to be Used for the Edification of the Church
 • Christ Purchased Our Gifts. Eph. 4:10
 • Christ Has Given Equipping Gifts
 • Gifts Are for Ministry
 • Ministry Builds Up the Body
III. Spiritual Gifts Are to Be Used for Ministry and Evangelism
 • The Priority of Ministry and Evangelism
 • Ministry Opens the Door for Evangelism.
 • Evangelism is the Ultimate Purpose for Ministry.
IV. Spiritual Gifts Are to be Used in a Complementary Way
 • The Competitive Spirit
 • The Complementary Spirit
V. Spiritual Gifts Will Be Accounted for at the Judgment Seat of Christ
 • Believers Are Responsible
 • Believers Are Accountable

Chapter Four

Getting a Grip
on Your Gifts

A church is like a football team with great capabilities. The football team has 11 outstanding athletes on the playing field. They huddle, and the quarterback calls the play. Every player knows his assignment well. If every team member executes his assignment correctly, a touchdown is guaranteed! But, suppose no one knows his position or his assignment on the plays. After the huddle, no one lines up. No one knows what to do! What will happen? Failure! The team will be decimated!

The church has many team members. Like the football team, it can be effective if each team member knows the plays and has mastered his or her assignment. This church team can powerfully carry out the mission of its Head, the Lord Jesus Christ. But, if members are unsure of what position to play and do not know where to line up, guess what will happen? Just like the losing football team, it will be defeated.

It is important that we know what to do with our spiritual gifts. Next, we will look at five biblical principles for using our spiritual gifts.

• Spiritual gifts are to be used, not left dormant   Rom. 12:6

• Spiritual gifts are to be used for the edification of the church 1 Cor. 14:12

• Spiritual gifts are to be used for ministry and evangelism Matt. 9:35-38

• Spiritual gifts are complementary 1 Cor. 12:20-23

• Spiritual gifts will be accounted for at the Judgment Seat of Christ   Rom. 14:10-14

PRINCIPLE ONE:
Spiritual Gifts Are to Be Used, Not Left Dormant
(Rom. 12:6)

The Father, the great Architect of the universe and Designer of every life, has given spiritual gifts to every person. The potential is within our genes at conception. Through the blood of the Divine Purchaser of our total beings, we have been bought with a price. We are not our own; we belong to Him! When we receive Christ, we are born of the Holy Spirit. We are not aware of the gifts and potential that lies within us. In the life of every believer is a reservoir of untapped resources. Gifts and clusters of gifts that give tremendous potential for service lie within us. The Holy Spirit works within us to surface whatever gifts are needed for us to obey Him in ministry and witness.

He has given us gifts. "Let us use them" (Rom. 12:6). Do not leave them dormant and unused. Whatever God desires for us to do, we can do! His will for us begins with the surrender of all we are and all we possess to Him. Obedience to the will of God is the key! When we step out in obedience to Him, it will surprise us what God can do through us.

God's Will Involves Our Gifts

God wants to use each of us! He wants to use every gift He has given us. He gave them to be used! This is His will for everyone!

"I beseech you therefore, brethren, by the mercies of God, that you present your bodies a living sacrifice, holy, acceptable to God, which is your reasonable service. And do not be conformed to this world, but be transformed by the renewing of your mind, that you may prove what is that good and acceptable and prefect will of God" (Rom. 12:1-2)

How can we know the will of God? How can we know what God wants us to do with our spiritual gifts? The answer lies in some general guidelines that are true for every person. In Romans 12:1-2 God gives us direction:

Keep your mind renewed through submission to God. The world wages a constant warfare to press us into its mold and keep us from having victory through His power. Yielding to the Holy Spirit moment by moment keeps on transforming us into persons who live abundantly. The New Testament Greek word for transform is "metamorpheo" from which comes our word "metamorphis." It means to "change over." It is the process by which a worm is transformed into a beautiful, soaring butterfly. We are continually changed by the Holy Spirit.

Trust God with your life. Do not fear His will. His will is:

Good—It is good for you and for everyone related to you in any way!

Acceptable—It is well suited! It fits just right! God's will is tailor-made just for you! Sometimes you can buy a suit that looks great when you purchase it. Later, when you wear it, you realize it doesn't fit. Then you recognize that you were captivated by its appearance, not its fit. When you wear it, you are uncomfortable. You feel that every eye is on you. But, when you go to a tailor and have a suit made just to fit, you feel at ease wearing the suit. It is tailor-made just for you! That is how God's will is for you. It fits just right! God tailored it just for you.

Perfect—It comes to completion! You will come out just right!

Yield your life to God and be willing to do His will. He will reveal it one step at a time.

As we become willing to do His will, He will lead us into the areas where He will use our gifts.

He will reveal His specific will to each individual. Then, He will provide whatever we need to obey Him. He will surface the gift in our lives that He wants us to use in His service.

However, if we are fearful or rebellious and will not step forward in obedience to Him, the gift or gifts will remain dormant within us. Sadly, we may never know we have a particular gift if we fail to trust and obey Him in attempting to do what He says.

Life is a great adventure as we walk in quiet obedience to His wonderful leadership. Nothing else can compare to the joy of realizing that we fit in the place where He has directed us. Nothing can be more satisfying than to be useful to the King of Glory in fulfilling His eternal purpose. Using your spiritual gifts for His glory is Kingdom Work that pays eternal dividends!

PRINCIPLE TWO:
Spiritual Gifts Are to Be Used for the Edification of the Church

"Even so you, since you are zealous for spiritual gifts, let it be for the edification of the church that you seek to excel" (1 Cor. 14:12)

The church of our Lord, the Body of Christ, is to use every spiritual gift for edification. The word "edify" means to build up. As a stone mason builds a great cathedral stone upon stone, the Lord Jesus Christ builds His church with living stones. The true cathedral of our Lord is not a building made of stone and mortar. The true church, the cathedral of our Lord, is *people*. Life upon life, our Lord builds His church. "On this rock *I will build My church*," Jesus declared (Matt. 16:18). The astounding fact is that He chooses to do it through human beings. All of us can have a part in building up His church! In fact, every believer is charged by our Lord to use our gifts to build up His Body.

Christ has given us gifts for that purpose. While it is enjoyable to exercise our gifts and feel fulfilled as a part of the Body, gifts are not to be used for our enjoyment and entertainment. While appreciation and respect may come as we use our gifts for the glory of Christ and to build up His Body, they are never for self-aggrandizement. While financial support may be given by the church to us as we use our gifts, they are not to be used for purposes of greed and financial advancement. Our spiritual gifts are to be used for the edification of the church.

The testimony of Bill Bright illustrates the right use of gifts for the edification of the church. In their early years, Bill and his wife, Vonette, had become believers. God spoke to their hearts about His will for them. God called them to evangelize the world for Christ. In 1951 they started Campus Crusade for Christ. They have done more to enlist and equip believers to reach people for Christ than practically anyone in our world today. As a result, multitudes around the world have come to know Christ because of their ministry. They have lived humbly and modestly and never sought recognition nor material things for themselves. Bill said that when he and Vonette committed their lives to Christ, they made a contract with God. In their contract they said, "As long as we live, we will be God's slaves." With no personal ambition and with an attitude of total availability to Christ, God has used them mightily.

Christ is the one who purchased our gifts. He is depicted in Ephesians 4:8-10 as the Conqueror who has defeated the enemy and has "led captivity captive" to give gifts to men. By His death, resurrection, and ascension, He has won the war for our souls and has purchased us with the price of His blood. We were captives! Now, He has freed us! As freed captives we are His own purchased possessions. We are born from above into His Kingdom! Each of us is gifted and is now freed to serve our Risen Lord. He has appointed persons He has gifted for leadership to equip each and every one of His "set-apart ones" to do the work of ministry for the building up of the Body of Christ.

Apostles, prophets, evangelists, pastors, and teachers are given special gifts to help outfit the entire church to be the Body of Christ on mission for Him. Every believer is to be equipped and enabled to do the work of "service" (in the Greek, *diakonias*). The work of service includes any and every work for our Lord in witnessing, reaching, ministering, discipling, and equipping people to follow Christ. Every Christian is a minister and is responsible to do the work of ministering. Gifts are used in ministering!

Then, a concluding purpose clause is given as the last phrase of Ephesians 4:12—"for the edifying (building up) of the body of Christ." The purpose of leaders equipping every member to minister is so that the Body will be built up. The Body of Christ is built up in two ways. One, it is built up in maturity as the people of God are taught, equipped and discipled. In this way the Body becomes strong and healthy. Two, the Body needs to be built up in number as believers witness and lead the lost to know Christ and to incorporate them into the life of the church. They must, then, be equipped to reach and disciple others. Thus, the Body of Christ is built up by all of the people of God being equipped and doing the work of the ministry.

PRINCIPLE THREE:
Spiritual Gifts Are to Be Used for Ministry and Evangelism

The church of our Lord Jesus Christ is a ministering/witnessing Body. It has a three-fold priority in mission:
1. Exalt the Savior
2. Equip the Saints
3. Evangelize the Sinner

The bottom-line purpose of Jesus for His church is people. Christ came for people! He spoke His word of purpose and passion when the religious leaders criticized Him for ministering to Zachaeus, the outcast tax collector. As they accused Him for going into the home of a man who was a "sinner," Jesus replied, "The Son of Man has come to seek and to save that which was lost" (Luke 19:10).

Christ went wherever people were to seek them and reach them for salvation. Reaching them begins with seeking those who are lost. He went among the masses and took time for the individual. "Then Jesus went about all the cities and villages, teaching in their synagogues, preaching the gospel of the kingdom, and healing every sickness and every disease among the people. But when He saw the multitudes, He was moved with compassion for them, because they were weary and scattered, like sheep having no shepherd. Then He said to His disciples, "The harvest truly is plentiful, but the laborers are few. Therefore pray the Lord of the harvest to send out laborers into His harvest" (Matt. 9:35-38).

The heart of Jesus beats for the souls of people. If the hearts of the followers of Jesus truly beat like the heart of the Master, they too will beat for souls. As Head of the church, His Body, He leads it to seek every lost person and guide them to salvation. Christ desires every follower to witness. He commanded every believer, "But you shall receive power when the Holy Spirit has come upon you; and you shall be witnesses to Me in Jerusalem, and in all Judea and Samaria, and to the end of the earth" (Acts 1:8). Witnessing is every Christian's job. Christ desires every person to be reached for Christ. Every Christian will need to be involved if every lost person is reached for Christ.

Christ gave Himself in caring ministry to people. Through His ministering, He taught us to care for people and reach them with the message of salvation. Nothing opens the door for witness for Christ more meaningfully than does loving people and ministering to them in the name of Jesus. In a church where I was pastor we organized a ministry to help people facing physical, emotional, family, financial, and other needs. As a pastor, I trained our people to share with people at the point of their need. I taught them how to guide a conversation by asking non-threatening questions and doing a lot of listening. As people began to open up and share their deeper needs, our people would share Christ with them and seek to lead them to Him.

O. E. Wilkins gave himself to that ministry, but he was limited in time because he had a part-time job to supplement his meager retirement income, and a chronic illness limited his physical activities. He, thus, appeared to be very limited in his gifts and abilities. Yet, he allocated two hours a day to minister to people. He would come to the church office every afternoon after three o'clock to pick up supplies to deliver to a poor family.

As his pastor, I taught O. E. as well as others how to ask questions, listen and dialogue through John 3:1-18 with a person or family. As he visited people or encountered them in his work, O. E. would do the simple things I had taught him. Sunday after Sunday O. E. would bring people to church that he had led to Christ the previous week. They would confess Christ, follow Him in baptism, and begin to serve our Lord.

Several years later after I had moved away to another church, I heard from O. E. through his pastor. By then he was even more limited. He could no longer work part-time. But, his new pastor said, "O. E. told me to express his love to you and tell you that he is still visiting with people and sharing John 3 with them." What tremendous joy that brought to my heart just to know that God can use every member and every gift to reach those who are lost.

God has equipped every member of the Body to both minister and witness. Christ has commissioned each local church to saturate its area with the gospel and to share Christ with every person in its geographical area and sphere of influence. This is the Acts 1:8 strategy of evangelism. This strategy has been delineated in my book, *Total Church Life* (published by Broadman & Holman Publishers), chapters 10 & 11. I call it "Total Evangelism." The concept of "Total Evangelism" involves a church in the "Total Penetration" of its area with the gospel of Christ through the "Total Participation" of its members in witnessing.

Every local church has an army capable of reaching its community in ministry and witness for Christ. It is the army of members in the church led by the pastor. Every member has received gifts from our Lord. These gifts are all to be used for evangelism, ministry and discipleship. Every gift is for evangelism! Each gift can be used to enhance the individual believer's witness for Christ and thereby increase the effectiveness of the corporate witness of the Body.

Evangelism is a passion! It is a fire burning within us! When we have the passion of Christ for reaching people, we will find a way to use any and every gift to share the Good News and lead others to know Him. A commitment to this priority will enable every member to be who he or she is and allow Christ to work through them. Every one is different. This the dynamic of evangelism. Every lost person is different, also! Consequently God uses each of us in different ways to reach out and to touch different people.

EVERY GIFT IS FOR EVANGELISM!!!!!

PRINCIPLE FOUR:
Spiritual Gifts Are to Be Used in a Complementary Way

Every gift is important. All the gifts in its members' lives need to be actively used in the Body to make it healthy and powerful in accomplishing the mission of Christ, the Head.

"For as the body is one and has many members, but all the members of that one body, being many, are one body, so also is Christ. For by one Spirit we were all baptized into one body—whether Jews or Greeks, whether slaves or free—and have all been made to drink into one Spirit. For in fact the body is not one member but many" (1 Cor. 12:12-14).

A church may emphasize spiritual gifts in ways that result in one of two different directions of ministry. Individual members can go in either of these two directions. One is when members use their spiritual gifts in a **competitive way.** The other is when they use their spiritual gifts in a **complementary way.**

The Competitive Way

The first, the competitive way, is marked best by individualism, with members focusing on their own gifts and promoting only what they do in the Body. Paul reproved the Corinthians about this. One member may not be aware of what other members of the Body are contributing. They are so focused on their own ministry they do not realize the value of the Body functioning as a unified team. This is especially a danger to new believers. They have such joy in coming to know Christ, knowing they have a home in Heaven, and experiencing the astounding reality that God can use them in His work that they are oblivious to what God is doing in the lives of others. These believers sometimes get so caught up in the ecstasy of what they are doing that they are not conscious of the effect they are having on the rest of the Body.

The Body is one body with many members who are interdependent and inter-related. None can be fully effective alone. Each needs the other. Each gift empowers the others synergistically. "There should be no schism in the body, but that the members should have the same care for one another. And if one member suffers, all members suffer with it; or if one member is honored, all the members rejoice with it" (1 Cor. 12:25-26).

When members ignore the biblical truth of unity in the Body, they become more individualistic in ministry. Some may move outside their church to start their own independent ministries. From these ministries the church may benefit but not nearly so powerfully as it would if the members matured and used their gifts together to build up the Body. God would use such members in a greater Kingdom way to benefit other churches if they would release their gifts to be used by their local church.

Even worse than spiritual immaturity is when the competitive way of using spiritual gifts is marked by carnality and selfish ambition. Ungodly and even non-believing members and leaders attempt to use the church for their own financial gain or personal power and glory. This was a problem in the Church of Corinth.

Paul makes a frontal attack on the pride problem of Corinth when he says, "If the foot should say, 'Because I am not the hand, I am not of the body,' is it therefore not of the body" (1 Cor. 12:15).

With his vivid imagination Paul describes the parts of a human body as if each part had a separate personality, could speak, and interact individually with other parts. He has the ear saying, "Because I am not an eye, I am not of the body." The eye says to the hand, "I have no need of you."

Pride causes self-centeredness that creates dissatisfaction in the hearts of members. It causes ambition that leads members to depreciate others and elevate themselves or to elevate others and depreciate themselves. This leads to position-seeking among members. Some members become angry and drop out if they do not get the position they desire. Others feel threatened by the success of those who are evidently being used greatly by God in the Body. Instead of "rejoicing with those who rejoice" and appreciating any ministry that builds up the Body, they criticize and attack other members to try to elevate themselves.

Used in a Complementary Way

Gifts are to be used in a complementary way. Members of the Body can remember that "God has set the members, each one of them, in the Body just as He pleased" (1 Cor. 12:18). God knows our gifts and where we can fit and be used best in the Body of Christ. It is critical that members be willing to allow God to use their gifts and appreciate the gifts of others.

Position-seeking decimates the Body. "But one and the same Spirit works all these things, distributing to each one individually as He wills" (1 Cor. 12:11). All members are needed! There is no unimportant member. Even the seemingly most insignificant member is essential to the life and work of the Body (1 Cor 12:2). *Everybody is somebody in the Lord's Body!* There is no Mr. Little or Mr. Big in the church. Every person is important. God wants to use each person with his or her gift. When members appreciate one another and "have the same care for one another" (1 Cor. 12:25), competition ceases, unity develops and the Body functions as a powerful team.

When the <u>church functions as a team</u>, the gifts of individual members become synergistic. Each is enhanced in its power and effectiveness. The witness of individual Christians is greatly strengthened, and the corporate witness of the Body has far-reaching effects.

Many more non-believers will be reached for Christ through team witnessing than through the independent witness of individual Christians.

It was a moving experience the Sunday Keith made his profession of faith. The pastor asked people who had in some way sought to reach him for Christ and had touched his life through a witness to come and stand with him as he was introduced to the church. Seventeen people came and joyfully surrounded him!

All of them had prayed for their lost friend. Three who had gifts of mercy sent Keith notes through the mail. One with a gift of giving had given him a Bible. Another with a gift of administration had made a suggestion that positively improved his business. In three years seven of them had visited him in his home. Two had taken him to ball games. Another had helped him with a home-repair project. Those who were instrumental in reaching him had gifts ranging from exhortation, mercy, teaching, giving, pastoring, prophecy, hospitality, administration, helps, to that of the evangelist. The person who had the gift of the evangelist was not the one who led the new believer to Christ. It was the person with the gift of administration who was used to draw the net and lead him through the conversion experience. God used this team of Christ's witnesses, whose gifts varied greatly, to do all that was humanly needed to help their friend to know and follow Jesus.

In every part of the church life gifts can be used to complement one another for greater power, influence, and effectiveness. *Spiritual gifts are meant to be used in a complementary way in the Body of Christ. They are Team Gifts!*

PRINCIPLE FIVE:
Spiritual Gifts Will Be Accounted for at Christ's Judgment Seat

Spiritual gifts are given by God to be used! They are grace endowments from God to the Body of Christ through individual members to be used for the edification of the church. As individual believers, we are responsible for the development and use of these gifts. We are accountable for what we do with them!

The scriptural admonition to use the gifts God has given us is clear. "For as we have many members in one body, but all the members do not have the same function, so we, being many, are one body in Christ, and individually members of one another. Having then gifts differing according to the grace that is given to us, let us use them" (Rom. 12:4-6).

We are stewards of all the gifts and resources within our possession. Everything we have and use belongs to God. We are managers of what He entrusts to us. This can be compared to the manager of a business. For example, McDonald's fast-food restaurant chain has spread worldwide. I have visited McDonald's in Bucharest, Romania; Sao Paulo, Brazil; Seoul, Korea; and many places in the United States. Wherever you go, their menus are the same. Wherever in the world it is located, a McDonald's restaurant will have a manager. The manager is responsible for what happens in that particular restaurant. He or she will give an account periodically to the owner. If the manager has done a good job and the restaurant has prospered, the person will be commended and rewarded. If he or she has done a poor job and the business has lost money, the manager will be reprimanded and may be fired. We are managers of God's resources and will report in to Him. "As each one has received a gift, minister it to one another, as good stewards of the manifold grace of God" (1 Pet. 4:10). "For we shall all stand before the judgment seat of Christ. For it is written: 'As I live says the Lord, Every knee shall bow to Me, and every tongue shall confess to God.' So then each of us shall give account of himself to God" (Rom. 14:10-12).

Jesus gave several parables to demonstrate the stewardship responsibility all people have. One of them is the Parable of the Talents in Matthew 25:14-30. In it He made it clear that all of us have received gifts (represented by "talents" which in that day referred to a sum of money) from God—some more and some less. We are only responsible for what we do with what we have, not what we have compared to what others have. One servant received five talents, another received two talents, and the third received one. The first two used theirs and doubled them. The third was filled with fear and took his one talent and buried it. He wanted to make sure he had it when the master returned.

On the day of the accounting the fearful servant said, "I was afraid, and went and hid your talent in the ground. Look, there you have what is yours."

"But his lord answered and said to him, 'You wicked and lazy servant,. . . you ought to have deposited my money with the bankers, and at my coming I would have received back my own with interest. Therefore take the talent from him, and give it to him who has ten talents. For to everyone who has, more will be given, and he will have abundance; but from him who does not have, even what he has will be taken away. And cast the unprofitable servant into the outer darkness. There shall be weeping and gnashing of teeth.'"

To the other servants who were faithful and obedient in using their talents and multiplying them the Lord said, "Well done, good and faithful servant; you were faithful over a few things, I will make you ruler over many things. Enter into the joy of your Lord."

It is a delight to know that every believer has gifts to use for our Lord. There is much to do in service for Him. In anything we do, we are using some gift God has given us. We have not only the responsibility to serve Him, but we have the privilege and joy of serving. *Our greatest joy will be our final reward—"Well done," from our Lord.*

ACTIVITIES

Discuss these questions in your study group or answer them personally:

1. Has there been a time when you obeyed Christ to seek to meet a need and a gift you did not know you had surfaced? What gift did you utilize?

_____

2. Had it been dormant until the Holy Spirit surfaced and anointed you to use it? Yes_____ No_____

3. How can gifts you think you have be used to edify the church?

_____

_____

_____

4. Why are all spiritual gifts to be used for ministry and evangelism?

_____

_____

_____

_____

5. Do you have a competitive or a cooperative attitude about using your gifts?   Yes_____   No_____

6. Do you feel that if the use of your gift is not superior to others, you will feel disappointed and inferior?   Yes_____   No_____

7. Are you willing to attempt whatever needs to be done for the glory of Christ and allow the Holy Spirit to surface gifts you didn't know you had?   Yes_____   No_____

Chapter Five

Sign Gifts in Action

Outline

Nineteen spiritual gifts are mentioned in the four major gift passages in the Bible. They may be categorized into three groups: Sign gifts; Support gifts; Service gifts.

I. Approaches to Understanding Sign Gifts
- Charismatic Approach
- Cessationist Approach
- Great Commission Approach

II. Miracles and Healings
- The Dynamic
  Instills Faith
  Affirms the gospel
- The Dangers
  Danger of Focus on Experiences Rather than Jesus
  Danger of Sensationalism
  Danger of Satan's Activity
  Danger of Denial

III. Tongues and Interpretation of Tongues
- The Purpose of Tongues
- The Perversion of Tongues
- The Procedures for Tongues
- The Possible Sources of Tongues
  God
  Satan
  Self-imposed Emotional and Psychological Experience

Chapter Five

Sign Gifts in Action

How many spiritual gifts are there? Who knows? What does the Bible say? Who is to decide? Is what I have a spiritual gift, a talent, or an ability? The questions seem endless when the subject of spiritual gifts arises.

The Bible does not explicitly answer many of our questions about spiritual gifts. But, whatever the answers may be, we can have confidence that we have whatever gift is needed for us to do what the Father wants us to do. Whatever is needed, our God will provide. Whether it is a gift, talent, or ability, the Holy Spirit will supply what we need. *Too much of a distinction has been made between gifts, talents, and abilities*. The distinction is not found in the Bible. The term "talent" has been used by some to explain gifts in the lives of nonbelievers. Regardless of the term used, whether what we have is a gift, talent, or ability, it came from a gracious God.

God, the Father, created every person for His purpose. At conception He endowed each of us with our personality, intelligence, and with the potential (ability, talent, gift, etc.) for whatever was needed to accomplish this purpose. *The potential for all we can become was stamped into our DNAs*. When we received Christ, the Holy Spirit entered our lives to surface gifts and to empower us to use them as they are needed. The gift, then, becomes a *spiritual* gift! Lost people have gifts from God. They become "spiritually directed and anointed" gifts when the person receives Christ as Savior and Lord. If a person rejects Christ, the potential for the spiritual gift will still be in that life. The latent gift potential will lie dormant or may be used for the good of society, but it will be without the Holy Spirit's anointing and empowerment.

As the year 2000 approached, *Time* magazine chose Albert Einstein as the most influential man during the 20th century. His scientific discoveries have greatly affected humanity. There is no question that Einstein was highly gifted by God.

A person may do humanitarian works to relieve the suffering of people and even do religious works yet not know Christ as Savior and Lord. The person may perform works for which he or she receives much attention and acclaim. These are like the people Jesus spoke about in Matthew 7 who had "done many wonderful works in His name but never knew Him."

The gifts God gives may even be used for evil purposes. Some gifted people can become so perverted that they, like Judas, are possessed and used by Satan. Like Judas, they may infiltrate the church where they feign spiritual gifts that are really counterfeit. Or, they may be gifts, but they are not Holy Spirit-directed and -empowered spiritual gifts. People such as Joseph Stalin and Adolf Hitler were highly gifted by God, but they rejected Him and used His gifts for evil purposes. Neither ever repented and received Christ; therefore, both were never led by the Holy Spirit. They are eternally lost.

Spiritual gifts enable us *to do what God wants us to do*. Obedience is the critical factor. If we live in Obedience to Christ, the Holy Spirit will surface the gift we need. The birth, baptism, indwelling, sealing, and filling of the Spirit distinctively makes us His children and empowers us to use His gifts in ministry. It is the fruit of the Spirit in our lives that gives evidence of our character within and of the qualities of Christ-likeness exhibited by our behavior. Both spiritual gifts and the fruit of the Spirit in our lives are essential for an effective life of service for Christ.

A LIST OF SPIRITUAL GIFTS FROM THE BIBLE

Students of spiritual gifts have arrived at different conclusions about how many actually exist. The numbers range from 18 up. As many as 27 have been suggested by different writers. Even though numerous spiritual gifts are mentioned, the Bible does not give us a specific number of how many there are.

As we search the Scriptures we find material on spiritual gifts in three major passages. Two lists are found in 1 Corinthians 12:6-8 and

28, one list is in Romans 12:6-8, and a third list of leadership gifts is located in Ephesians 4:11 In addition 1 Peter 4:9-10 offers an overview. In these four passages 19 gifts are listed. Paul pointed out basic gifts that would be used for the fulfilling of the mission of the church through the centuries ahead. In the Scriptures God gave gifts for activities and ministries that would be needed for Christ's mission. Much material has been written about gifts, and some lists attempt to name all the spiritual gifts. Reflecting the time in which they were compiled, some lists include celibacy and martyrdom.

In this book, we will focus on these four passages and draw from them a list of 19 definite biblical gifts. In these four passages 11 gifts are named only once. The gift of the prophet is listed four times and that of teacher is listed three times. In each of the passages that speak about gifts, the people of God are encouraged to submit whatever they have to Christ, the Head of the church, to use to build up His Body. Everything we do in service to Christ, we do using spiritual gifts from God which the Holy Spirit has surfaced to enable us to meet a particular need. When we act in obedience to the Holy Spirit, He directs us in the use of the gift. When we yield to the control of the Holy Spirit, He fills us and anoints us to use our spiritual gifts. What a difference this makes! Without the direction, fullness, and anointing of the Spirit, we use our gifts on our own strength. When we serve in the energy of the flesh, it is laborious and a heavy load to bear. It becomes so heavy that burnout will likely result.

In this study we will focus on the 19 gifts about which we are sure because the Bible has clearly identified them. The question is often asked if more gifts may exist than are listed in the Bible. The day in which we live is a different day from those during which the church was founded. Is it possible that God is giving gifts today that did not exist in New Testament times?

Grave problems arise with the claim that additional gifts exist than those named in the Scriptures. To list more gifts than those given in the Bible would be adding to the Word of God. This would amount to extra-biblical revelation. It would open the door for anyone to claim anything as a spiritual gift. Therefore, I have chosen to list and examine only those gifts specified in God's Word.

The following lists the spiritual gifts named in the Bible and the passages where they can be found:

From Ephesians 4:11; 1 Cor. 12:6-8; 12:28 Romans 12:6-8 and 1 Peter 4:9-10

Apostle
Prophet (Prophecy)
Evangelist
Pastor
Teacher (Teaching)
Word of Wisdom
Word of Knowledge
Faith
Miracles
Healings
Helps Ministering
Exhortation
Giving
Administration (Leading)
Mercy
Discerning of Spirits
Tongues
Interpretation of Tongues
Hospitality

These 19 gifts listed above are for the building up of the Body of Christ. They can be categorized according to the ways they may be used in the Body. They fall into three categories: Sign Gifts, Support Gifts, and Service Gifts.

Sign Gifts are those that involve the supernatural intervention of God in their usage. Today, they are the least utilized of all the gifts. **Support gifts** are those used in equipping and training members of the Body in using their gifts and in helping them to fulfill their ministries. They can be divided into two categories according to how they are used: First, some support gifts are used for equipping members for ministry and witness regardless of their gift. Second, others are used for enabling members of the Body to use their gifts powerfully. **Service gifts** are those used directly in ministry, witnessing, and activities that fulfill the mission of the Body.

SIGN GIFTS	SUPPORT GIFTS	SERVICE GIFTS
Miracles	*EQUIPPING*	Ministry/Service/Helps
Healing	Apostles	Exhortation
Tongues	Prophets	Administration/Leadership
Interpretation	Evangelists	Mercy
of Tongues	Pastors	Giving
	Teachers	\Hospitality
	ENABLING	
	Faith	
	Discernment	
	Wisdom	
	Knowledge	

The Sensational Sign Gifts

Sign is a word that comes from the New Testament Greek term *"semeion"*, which is usually translated "miracle." Sign gifts are the most controversial of all the gifts. This is because they involve the direct, supernatural intervention of God as they are used. Generally, God works through gifted believers in more natural ways. Consequently, the use of sign gifts is not as usual as that of support or service gifts. Today, believers are divided into three camps over the legitimacy of sign gifts. The three major approaches to understanding sign gifts are 1) the charismatic, 2) the cessationist, and 3) the Great Commission.

Charismatic Approach. Charismatic (neo-Pentecostal) believers contend that all sign gifts exist and are valid today. But, charismatics are divided over other issues regarding these gifts. Some charismatics believe that gifts are given through a second work of grace and that speaking in tongues is evidence of the baptism of the Holy Spirit. Some who hold this position claim that speaking in tongues is essential for salvation. This sometimes leads to emotional excess and sensationalism. Other charismatics hold that all gifts are valid today, but they reject the idea that tongues or any other gift is evidence of the fullness of the Holy Spirit.

Cessationist Approach. Cessationist believers hold the position that not all gifts are valid today. They believe that sign gifts are not legitimate and should not be exercised today. They have concluded that these gifts were given to the early church to validate the authority of those who had the gift. According to Cessationists, sign gifts ended with the completion of the writing of the Scriptures and its canonization. The biblical passage used to justify this position is 1 Corinthians 13:8-10. Some interpret verse 10 ("But when that which is perfect has come") to refer to the canonization of Scripture. They believe "that which is in part will be done away" (verse 10 also) refers to the sign gifts and "tongues" in particular. However, included in the list of gifts Paul mentioned in the context of the passage are not only tongues but also prophecy and knowledge. If we take the entire chapter, faith would be included among the gifts that are no longer valid. My own understanding is "when that which is perfect has come" will be when we are with Christ and we will "see face-to-face." Now, "we see through a glass darkly." This passage is misapplied to invalidate sign gifts today.

Great Commission Approach. Sign gifts are valid today although not as prominent as in New Testament times. The main purpose in the early church for the sign gifts was to substantiate the gospel. The ability to speak the gospel in other languages and the performing of miracles legitimized and enhanced the spreading of the gospel and effect in the lives of lost people. It was for enhancing and spreading of the gospel that miracles were done in the ministries of the apostles. These were done through the ministries of Peter and John in the healing of the lame man at the Beautiful Gate of the Jewish temple in Acts 3 and the raising of Dorcas from the dead in Acts 9. Special miracles were given by God through Paul in Acts 20:11. These reinforced the truth of the effect of the gospel of Christ. Because we have the Scriptures, the need for miracles to substantiate the gospel is not as great today as then. Today we have the full canon of the Scriptures, the church has been developed, and the spread the gospel is worldwide. The Holy Spirit is doing His work to empower the gospel to reach those who are without Christ. However, there are times and places today where the miraculous interventions of God are still needed for the impact of the gospel. When God chooses, He surfaces those gifts today for the glory of Christ and the salvation of the lost. He does so through the lives of those He has chosen as human instruments as they obey Him in ministry.

To understand the use of sign gifts is to view them in the light of the commission of Christ. In the statement of the Great Commission in Mark 16:15-18 Jesus said, "Go into all the world and preach the gospel to every creature." Then, He said, "And these signs will follow those who believe: In My name they will cast out demons; they will speak with new tongues; they will take up serpents; and if they drink anything deadly, it will by no means hurt them; they will lay hands on the sick, and they will recover"(Mark 16:17-19).

If we will obey His commission, He will do whatever is necessary to enable us to take the gospel to every creature. If demons oppose and get in the way, God will give the power to cast out the demons. If we cannot communicate with those who need Christ, He will give the power to communicate even if it is to miraculously speak with languages we have not learned. If snakes bite us, they won't hurt us. This happened to Paul on the Island of Malta (Acts 28:3-7), and God protected him. If we drink something poisonous or polluted, God will protect us from harm. Missionaries of our Lord have eaten and drunk things that would have poisoned them, but God protected them. Recently I read such a story. Missionaries in a pagan area were given poisonous food by the enemies of Christ. It did not affect them. The entire village turned to Christ because of this miracle. God will do whatever it takes to enable His people to take the gospel to every creature.

According to some scholars Mark 16:9-20 is not in some of the earliest manuscripts of the gospel of Mark. However, it is in most of them. But when it is interpreted in the light of Jesus' emphasis in Mark 16:15 (a statement of the Great Commission), then and only then does it harmonize with the Spirit of Christ and the rest of His teachings. The problem is some have taken verses out of context and used them as a basis for non-biblical religions. For example some use only a clause from this passage make a religion out of baptismal regeneration. Others have created religions out of speaking in unknown tongues, snake handling, etc.

False claims about sign gifts and their misuse have caused many believers to hesitate to accept anything that claims to be a supernatural occurrence. We can go to an extreme either way. The key is to maintain a scriptural balance through teaching the Word and obeying Christ.

MIRACLES AND HEALINGS

These gifts are abilities to be used of God in mighty, supernatural works and occurrences that glorify Christ and build up His Body. The exercise of these gifts both in the New Testament and through church history until now has not been the norm. The gift of miracles and healings surfaces only occasionally as God, the Father, chooses to supernaturally intervene into the affairs of men through the ministry of an individual or a church body.

Many cripples were in the temple area when Peter and John went to pray and encountered the lame man at the Beautiful Gate. God chose to intervene and do a miraculous work in healing the man. As a result, a great crowd gathered, and Peter proclaimed Christ to them. About 5,000 men besides the women and children were saved. This was tremendous! But, he was the only crippled person in the temple area at that time to experience a miracle.

Individual believers are gifted and used by God in His mighty works but not on a continuing basis. In New Testament times, signs and miracles were done sporadically even through the lives of the Apostles. Then and today God has surfaced these gifts at times of need for the confirmation of the gospel to an individual or a group. God has no doubt gifted individuals for physical healing. In some cases God heals through direct intervention, but in most it is through the understanding of how to cooperate with God's natural laws that healing comes. The medical field has made such great advances that today what occurs would have been thought miraculous 50 years ago. Surely God gives the spiritual gift of healing to some in the medical field to enable them to minister so that healing results. It is not always easy to discern the dividing line between natural and supernatural healing. After all, no healing occurs apart from the activity of God. God heals both through natural processes and supernatural intervention.

God still chooses to intervene in human affairs as it pleases Him and to use human instrumentality to reveal His love and power. God can do anything! God can still do anything! God can give the power to whomever He chooses to perform miraculous works.

The Dynamic of Miracles and Healings

The dynamic of the gifts of miracles and healings is that it instills faith into the life of the church and the lives of individuals as God does His mighty works. The people of God trust Him and gain the courage to step out in obedience to do whatever the Father calls them to do. They know that they can depend on Him. He will bring about what needs to happen and do what needs to be done. This results in the church being Spirit filled and Spirit directed.

As the Apostolic Period came to a close and the New Testament was being completed, the written Word was available to authenticate the ministry and message of Christ and the Apostles. Subsequently, history verifies a slowing down of the use of "sign gifts" to confirm the gospel to the unbelievers. John Bisagno, former pastor of First Baptist Church, Houston, Texas, has given much time and effort to world missions. In his book, *Charismatic Theology Under the Searchlight,* he suggests that today in pagan countries where there is no knowledge of and faith in the message of the New Testament, it is not unusual for missionaries to report the mighty works of God.

God still uses the miraculous sign gifts to confirm the gospel when needed. They affirm the authenticity of the message of God's salvation by grace through faith in Jesus Christ. But history reveals the more exposure people have to the Word, the less they need to validate its truth with miraculous signs. The Holy Spirit performs His own validation in the heart of the person who hears the Word.

The Dangers in Sign Gifts

Several dangers surround the issue of the sign gifts.

The first danger is the possibility of taking our eyes off the Lord and focusing on experiences. With an overemphasis on signs and miracles, people can become miracle seekers rather than obedient disciples of our Lord. When this occurs, miracles may be reported that never actually happen. People begin to see the miraculous in everything that occurs.

The second danger is the possibility of sensationalism and emotionalism. Individuals and churches may resort to using schemes to manufacture exciting and emotion-producing events to give the appearance of the mighty works of God. This results in a lack of integrity within the church that drains it of its spiritual vitality.

The third danger is that of Satan's activity. When people become enamored with the miraculous and try to manufacture miracles, Satan takes advantage of such pride and carnality. He will deceive through counterfeit miracles and gain control of the lives of scripturally and spiritually ignorant people.

Any or all of these dangers can begin to happen in a church that ceases to follow biblical authority and begins to make experience its authority. Such a church will soon lose its spiritual and doctrinal integrity. It will lose its witness in the community by discrediting its authenticity. Such a group may keep the name church, but not be a true Body of Christ. Like Jesus warned the church of Ephesus, "Remember therefore from where you have fallen; repent and do the first works, or else I will come to you quickly and remove your lamp-stand from its place—unless you repent" (Rev. 2:5).

The fourth danger is denial of the miraculous altogether. This can lead to a person-centered church that depends not on the Holy Spirit but human ingenuity and organization. Some are so fearful of the extremism and excesses of others that they restrict the work of the Holy Spirit. This kind of attitude and spirit kills churches. Dead churches have forgotten who God is and what He can do.

TONGUES AND THE INTERPRETATION OF TONGUES

Of all the gifts, the issue surrounding that of tongues has been the most volatile. This grows out of a misunderstanding of the Book of Acts and 1 Corinthians. The legitimate gift of tongues is found in the Book of Acts. This gift provides the ability to speak and communicate the gospel in another language. The interpretation of tongues is the ability to understand a language and convey its meaning to others. These two gifts are closely related.

"And they were all filled with the Holy Spirit and began to speak with other tongues as the Spirit gave them utterance . . . .. Then they were all amazed and marveled, saying to one another, 'Look, are not all these who speak Galileans? And how is it that we hear, each in our own language in which were born?'" (Acts 2:4,7,8) Clearly this was the miraculous communication of the gospel in languages that the believers had not learned. The gift of tongues occurred again at the home of Cornelius in Acts 10:44-48 as a sign to substantiate that Gentiles, too, are included in God's plan of salvation through Christ. Again, at Ephesus in Acts 19:6 after Paul had taught converts fully about salvation through Christ and the ministry of the Holy Spirit, they spoke with tongues and prophesied.

The Purpose of Tongues Is To Reach the Lost

The purpose of tongues was, first and foremost, to reach the lost for Christ. Second, included in the purpose is the fact that the gift of tongues was given to provide a sign to Jewish believers that the gospel is for both Jews and Gentiles. Pagans are included in God's plan. Jewish believers had a difficult time comprehending the width and breadth of the gospel. They would have been content for Christianity to be simply another sect within Judiasm. But Christ very clearly came with a gospel for the entire world! After His resurrection, He continued to move through the Holy Spirit and through His interventions in the church to break down these old barriers. By giving the supernatural ability to speak in tongues to the first Gentile converts as the Holy Spirit initially came upon them, Jesus substantiated the fact that the gospel is for both Jews and Gentiles. The gospel quickly spread around the world just as Jesus had commissioned in Acts 1:8.

The question naturally arises, "Does God still give the gift of tongues for the communication of the gospel?" The answer is, "Yes. When the ability to speak in another language to communicate the gospel in order to bring a person to Christ occurs, God gives that ability." Many reports substantiate that this can and does happen.

Aaren Gushwa, who serves as a director of missions in the U.S. Northwest, shares the following incident: "While visiting with an elderly man in our church, he told me of an experience that he had many years ago as a young man. While working as a janitor at a tuberculosis hospital, he stepped outside into the courtyard, where he noticed a young Hispanic woman weeping. He approached her and asked if there was anything he could to help.

The young women replied that her younger brother was dying of tuberculosis, and she was frightened. He began to speak words of comfort, and it resulted in her receiving Christ. They hugged and left each other. The next day he met the young woman again. But this time he was unable to communicate with her. She could speak only Spanish and he could speak only English.

She went away frustrated. After a while she returned with a nurse who could speak Spanish. Through the nurse he learned that the young woman did not understand why he could not speak Spanish. Just the day before she had heard him speak perfect Spanish. He replied with amazement that he had heard her speak in perfect English.

The elderly man looked at me and said, "Pastor, I don't know if I spoke Spanish or she spoke English. But, I do know that the Holy Spirit brought understanding for us both. Pastor, that, was the gift of tongues."

Dr. Preston Nix, pastor of Eastwood Baptist Church, Tulsa, OK, offers a similar story. One of his members, a relatively new Christian, went on a mission trip to Nova Iguacu just outside of Rio de Janeiro, Brazil.

"From the moment we stepped off the plane, it was evident God was with us. But (it was) never so evident as the day my interpreter and I had an appointment to meet and witness to the husband of a lady who attended the church. After a brief visit with the church member, she directed us outside where her husband was talking to a neighbor. We introduced ourselves and started telling the two about Jesus. The neighbor, not wanting anything to do with the topic of conversation, left for home.

As we continued to witness to the gentleman, a young girl of about 19 or 20 walked up and stopped to listen to our conversation. She didn't say anything. She just stood there and hung on every word. The man, however, only wanted to argue and debate every point we made. After 15 or 20 minutes, my interpreter wasn't even including me in the debate anymore. She was so wrapped up in trying to prove her point that she completely forgot about me. Not understanding a word they were saying, I bowed my head and began to pray. "God, What can we say to this man, and why are we here doing this?"

Then, in my frustration, I blurted out, "But wouldn't you like the assurance that if you died tonight, you would go to be with Jesus in heaven?"

As I finished asking my question, I looked up into the face of the young girl on the sidewalk. With tears in her eyes she said, "I want that assurance."

You could have knocked me over with a feather. Not only did this young lady want to receive Jesus, but she could speak English. I bolted over to her and asked if she would like to pray to receive Jesus as her Savior. To my surprise she didn't understand a word I was saying or visa versa.

A little confused by what had just taken place, I pried my interpreter away from the debate. Together we prayed with the young lady as she accepted the free gift of salvation. As we stood there crying and hugging, I realized that God had placed us there for her. She didn't even live there. She was visiting a friend and was just passing by. But, even more incredible, for just a moment God lifted the language barrier long enough to catch my attention so this young girl 100 miles from home could receive Christ into her heart and life.

Perversion of Tongues

By the time Paul wrote the First Corinthians, a change had already occurred in the practice of speaking in tongues. The Corinthian believers were duplicating a pagan practice of speaking in unintelligible sounds. This had become a severe problem which Paul addressed in 1 Corinthians 14. The circumstances surrounding it had brought confusion and division into the church. It is not surprising that this highly gifted, but carnal, church was the only one about which such problems were recorded in the New Testament. The pagan culture influenced the church and added to the problem. The Corinthian church is the only one about which the Scriptures record any indication of the practice of ecstatic utterances or "unknown tongues."

I Corinthians 14 was not written to teach the practice of tongues. Paul wrote it for the purpose of correcting the Corinthian perversion of the true biblical gift of tongues. One of our problems today is that some have misapplied the passage to support non-scriptural teachings. They have chosen to use the passage to teach the very things that Paul was forbidding.

To understand tongues as practiced in Corinth, it necessary to examine the culture, history, and geography of the city and the church. The city of Corinth was located on a narrow isthmus of land between the Adriatic and the Aegean Seas. Today, a canal joins the two seas. As you arrive in the area, you cross a bridge and see a canal hundreds of feet below dug between two banks that form a deep ravine. When Paul ministered and started the church in Corinth, there was no canal. Instead, a wooden chute was constructed that extended across the narrow strip of land. It was kept slick with oil so that ships could be pulled through it by slave labor from one sea to the other. It was a harbor city where sailors waited between voyages. Corinth had the all the characteristics of such a seaport city—prosperity, drunkenness, gambling, prostitution, brawling, etc.

The pagan religious practices, also, contributed to the situation. On the top of the mountain south of Corinth stood a pagan temple dedicated to the Greek sex goddess, Aphrodite. Worshippers of this pagan goddess engaged in sexual intercourse as a part of their worship. Worship was led by priestess/prostitutes who incorporated speaking in tongues (ecstatic utterances) as a part of the emotional frenzies in their immoral, idolatrous worship. The priestess/prostitutes descended on the city at night and on holidays to engage in sexual activity with the sailors and local profligates.

This is the backdrop for Paul's instruction about dealing both with tongues and women's behavior in the church at Corinth. The church at Corinth had evidently elevated tongues to the place of supremacy among the gifts. In 1 Corinthians 14 Paul very patiently and tenderly instructed them in such a way as to regulate the practice. If Paul's instructions were followed, the practice would fade out of existence. Without condemning or setting up barriers that would alienate them, he tried to help the Corinthian believers think through what they were doing.

Paul's Procedures for Tongues

Note the following truths given by Paul:

14:1—Love is superior to every gift. Love is the test for validating everything we do. We are to "pursue love." Love is the quality that exceeds all gifts. If practiced without love any gift is worthless. "Though I speak with the tongues of men and angels, but have not love, I have become sounding brass or a clanging cymbal" (1 Cor. 13:1).

14:2—The tongues speaker does not speak to people but to God. People cannot understand what is said. He or she is speaking mysteries. If a person is doing it to speak to God, then, do it privately.

14:1-3—Prophecy is superior to tongues because it edifies, encourages and comforts hearers. Those who promote and elevate "tongues" claim that it is the supreme gift rather than love and prophecy. Without Scriptural support they claim that it is the evidence of the baptism of the Holy Spirit. It is looked on as the benchmark for spiritual greatness and the evidence of God's approval. Spiritual superiority is claimed by many who have "spoken in tongues", and those who have not are looked down upon as spiritually inferior.

14:4—Tongues speaking is self-centered. The tongues speaker builds up self. The one who prophesies builds up the church.

14:6-9—Tongues is like speaking into the air. It is better to speak "words easy to understand." The Corinthian style of tongues is compared with a "trumpet that sounds an uncertain sound." It makes no sense and will create confusion.

14:10-1—You should speak words that can be understood; otherwise there is no communication and no value in speaking.

14:12—If you want to excel, be zealous for gifts that will edify the church rather than for tongues which edify yourself.

14:13-19—Paul said that he spoke in tongues more than any of the Corinthians. But in church it is better to speak five words spoken with understanding than 10,000 in an "unknown" tongue. He did not indicate whether he spoke in languages or unintelligible speech. Whatever his experience was, he did not encourage others to do it nor teach others to do it. He did not claim spiritual superiority because of it. Whatever it was, he did it privately. He instructs those who are determined to speak in tongues to pray in order to be able to interpret.

14:20-21—Those who elevate tongues as the supreme gift are like rebellious "children" in need of spiritual maturity.

14:22-25—The original tongues gift was "a miracle for reaching the non-believer." The Corinthian "style of tongues" confuses the non-believer. Prophecy can be understood by non-believers and is beneficial to them.

14:26-33—Tongues are to be regulated.

Those who speak in tongues are not under the control of a force outside of themselves. They are responsible for their behavior. They can control what they do and say, and they are accountable for it. Anything done in church should be orderly and done for the building up of the body.

If tongues are spoken, it should be done by no more than two or three, with each speaking in turn. One must interpret. If there is no one to interpret for the benefit of the hearers, keep silent or speak to God alone.

14:39-40—"Do not forbid to speak with tongues. Let all things be done decently and in order."

The legitimate gift of tongues is the supernatural ability to communicate the gospel in a language not previously known. It is what happened in Acts 2. The Corinthian tongues were altogether different. Paul dealt kindly with the issue of "unknown" tongues in 1 Corinthians 14. But he regulated its usage in such a way that if practiced as he taught, it would fade out of existence or the practice would not be a hindrance in the Body.

Many will ask, "How do you explain the existence of tongues as they are being practiced today in the use of unintelligible, ecstatic utterances?" Apparently genuine believers have been involved in the practice of this type of tongues speaking. We, like Paul, need to have the Spirit of Christ and relate to them with kindness and generosity while emphasizing what he taught in the Word.

Three Possible Sources for Tongues Today

These three possible explanations for the spiritual experience of speaking in tongues today exist:

1. God
2. Satan
3. A self-imposed or other-influenced emotional/psychological experience.

Let's examine all three to see which one is more likely.

First, God is the source of all genuine spiritual experiences. No question lingers about God being the source of the tongues experiences in the Book of Acts. However, Scripture offers no indication that God gave the Corinthians tongues. There is no biblical evidence that the ecstatic/unknown tongues of today are from God. Some claim a prayer language. It is possible but not certain that Paul did this (1 Cor. 14:18-19). It is also possible that he spoke the gospel in other known languages. If he spoke in unintelligible words, he did it privately and not publicly because he did not consider it to be a practice that would edify the Body. He taught them to speak words that could be understood (vv. 13-19).

The second possible source of this spiritual experience is Satan. I have no doubt that in Corinth Satan inspired people to speak in and elevate "unknown" tongues. He is the author of confusion. Paul had to write three chapters (1 Cor. 12-14) to try to correct the severe problems that resulted. Satan works to divert and distract the church today from its unity and mission by elevating prideful and self-seeking people in the church. He gives experiences that "puff-up" with pride and create a spirit of condescension. He leads people into heresies to cause them to depart from the pure gospel. Because of such problems Paul went on to present the essence of the true gospel in 1 Corinthians 15.

The third possible source of this spiritual experience is that it was an emotional/psychological experience that is self-imposed or influenced by others. There's no doubt this happened at Corinth, where believers heard prominent members elevate the tongues experience. They sought "the gift." It happens today! In some groups where it is practiced, those who do not participate are told or made to feel that they are spiritually inferior or in some cases that they are not saved. They seek "the gift" and impose on themselves the psychological/emotional experience involved in tongues. Some groups teach their followers how to begin and practice saying unintelligible words, then to relax and make these sounds until the "gift" is happening. Is that wrong? Paul sought to regulate such activity in I Corinthians 14. He told them to "be zealous for gifts that edify the church" Is it healthy? Paul said that those who practiced tongues at Corinth "built up themselves." Some may experience a spiritual lift by such a practice in private. This could have been one of the reasons Paul said not to forbid it. Another reason may well be that he did not want to add to the chaos and disunity that already existed in the church by giving them something else to fight about.

Already some of the strong-willed, proud, carnal Corinthians were questioning Paul's apostleship and authority. If he had taken a strong, confrontational approach, he risked their total rejection of his influence. Therefore, he reasoned with them tenderly, attempting to establish boundaries to control the practice. If they followed his counsel, eventually the practice of unknown tongues would cease.

Balance Is the Key in Using Spiritual Gifts

The elevated emphasis on "sign gifts" during the past century has led to many excesses, misunderstandings, and even rejection of the idea of spiritual gifts by some. When the term "spiritual gifts" is used, many think of the excesses they have observed through the emphasis on sign gifts. Others are caught up in the desire for sensational experiences. Consequently the utilization of spiritual gifts in our ordinary, everyday lives has been neglected.

Some groups have gone too far with their emphasis on sign gifts. They have discredited themselves and the teachings about spiritual gifts not only with the world but also with many other believers. Satan has taken advantage and used the situation to create disunity in the general Body of Christ. This has resulted in distortion of the teachings of Scripture.

Consequently, because some have gone too far into excessive sensationalism—claiming they are practicing "the gifts"—others have almost totally rejected any emphasis at all on gifts. When this happens, believers often become rigid, suspicious and self-protective. They tend to de-emphasize the doctrine and work of the Holy Spirit. Their worship lacks joy, excitement, and vitality. Their lives and witness have no supernatural power. Their churches become dead and formal. Members begin to leave and attach themselves to groups which express joy and excitement though they may be biblically unsound.

We must find a balance where spiritual gifts are concerned. Because some have perverted the doctrines of the Holy Spirit and of spiritual gifts, we do not need to avoid the teaching and practice of these truths. God is at work! He wants to use each of us and each of our gifts in a powerful way to reach the lost for Christ and to build up His Body.

ACTIVITIES

Discuss the following in your study group or do them personally:

1. Have you familiarized yourself with the four passages where gifts are listed? _____ yes. _____ no. If not, do so now.

2. How are "sign gifts" related to the Great Commission?

_____

_____

_____

3. What dynamics do miracles and healing bring to the Body of Christ?

_____

_____

_____

4. What is a danger in exercising the gifts of miracles and healing?

_____

_____

_____

5. List four ways Paul regulated the Corinthian practice of tongues.

(1) _____

(2) _____

(3) _____

(4) _____

Chapter Six

Support Gifts
Equip and Enable
Outline

Support gifts are used to undergird the use of all gifts to build up the Body of Christ. There are two groups of support gifts—Equipping Gifts and Enabling Gifts.

I. Equipping Gifts Eph. 4:11-12
- Gift of the Apostle
- Gift of the Prophet
- Gift of the Evangelist
- Gift of the Pastor
- Gift of the Teacher

II. Enabling Gifts
- Gift of Faith
- Gift of Discernment
- Gift of Wisdom
- Gift of Knowledge

Chapter Six

Support Gifts
Equip and Enable

Support gifts are foundational in the building up of the Body of Christ. They undergird the use of all the gifts, and they are involved in all the ministries. They operate in two ways: First, they equip the people of God for the work of ministry. Second, they enable or strengthen believers who have been equipped to accomplish their ministry. The enabling gifts strengthen and empower all other gifts.

The equipping gifts often are the focal point of the church. They are the most highly visible of the gifts as they are exercised. They are essential for the building up of the church. These are the leadership gifts used for equipping all of the people of God. If the members who possess these gifts do their jobs faithfully, the work of the church can be accomplished. If these members lose sight of their purpose and simply try to do the work of ministry themselves rather than equipping and involving all the members, the church will not accomplish its mission. The purpose of these God-called leaders is to equip all of the people of God for ministry and witness (Eph. 4:11-12).

The pastor is to be the leader who shepherds and gives oversight to the church (Acts 20:28). As such he is the primary leader in equipping the saints. For a more complete explanation, see Chapter 5 in my earlier book, *Total Church Life*, published by Broadman & Holman Publishers, Nashville, Tennessee.

The hope of fulfilling Christ's mission is in the ministry involvement of all the people. Their effectiveness depends on how well they are equipped. The answer is the New Testament pattern of pastor and other church leadership persons devoting themselves to the equipping of believers. No way exists for those who have leadership support gifts to do all the work of the church alone. They can and need to do some of it as role models, but their great contribution is their enlisting, equipping, and engaging the members of the Body.

EQUIPPING GIFTS

Equipping gifts are listed in Ephesians 4:11. These are apostles, prophets, evangelists, pastors, and teachers.

GIFT OF THE APOSTLE

The word apostle (Greek—*apostolos*) means "one who is sent." The title was used for the original "Twelve Apostles" but was also used beyond that to include others who knew Jesus in the flesh. Paul, who met the risen Lord on the road to Damascus, was called an apostle. One of the requirements for a book to be included in the Canon of the New Testament was for it to have been written by an apostle or a companion of an apostle. In that sense there were no apostles after those who had been with Jesus died.

However, many believe that there is an apostle ministry today. It does not include the authority of receiving revelations and writing Scripture. But, they are "sent from God on a special mission." Apostles are sent out on mission from God with a gift for crossing cultural barriers and starting churches. They are usually missionaries and church planters who have the ability to start churches and exercise the general leadership of churches. Their authority in spiritual matters is spontaneously recognized and appreciated by those churches.

Dynamic:

The gift of the apostle is used in cross-cultural missions to plant churches in areas where Christianity is unknown or has not made a strong impact. The apostle has the ability to relate to non-believers, pagans, and people of non-Christian religions. The apostle effectively shares the gospel to secure their interest, lead them to Christ, and involve them in beginning a Christian church.

Every gift is for evangelism! The gift of the apostle offers a special ability to evangelize. Those with this gift must be equipped and have a passion to reach the lost. Their gift becomes effective to the extent that it is evangelistic. Without evangelism it is impossible to start new churches and to be effective in mission work.

Description:

An apostle must have vision for what God will do in expanding His work.

The characteristics of an apostle include:

• Faith to believe God in difficult circumstances.

• Ingenuity to perceive opportunities for penetrating an area and a social/cultural group with the gospel.

• Creativity and flexibility to attempt new and sometimes unusual methods in reaching people and starting churches.

• Administrative ability to lead in setting up the organization of a church.

• Persistence to stay with the task.

• Evangelistic ability to personally lead the lost to know Christ and to equip and inspire new believers to share Christ.

Difficulties:

A person with the gift of the apostle can become unrealistic in vision and nonproductive by emphasizing creativity to the neglect of basic growth principles and not caring for details. He may have difficulty in delegating and may tend to become impersonal in evangelism. The gift of the apostle enables one to be effective in church-starting, but not necessarily to pastor the church as it grows. He may lead a church to a certain size, then have difficulty in helping it to continue to grow.

Dangers:

Satan attacks the apostle at numerous points. Finances are a critical factor. Enough money never exists. The church planter who cares often puts money for personal and family living into the work being done. Personal, financial, and family problems can result. The apostle sometimes has a tendency to prefer to work alone and become aloof rather than be a team player. Burnout is always a danger due to the vision, intensity, and commitment of the church planter.

Delight:

The gift of the apostle enables the church to have the joy of helping to start new churches and of sending missionaries from their membership. Evangelism is expanded through the expansion of the Kingdom of God by starting new churches.

Do You Think You Have the Gift of the Apostle?

On a scale of one to 10, with one the least and 10 the greatest, respond to the following questions:

_____ To what extent do you think you have the gift of the apostle?

_____ To what extent are you exercising this gift as you follow Christ.

List the ways you are practicing the use of the gift of the apostle.

_____

_____

_____

List the ways you believe God wants you to exercise the gift of the apostle.

_____

_____

_____

GIFT OF THE PROPHET

Definition:

The prophet is one who receives God's truth and has the ability to publicly communicate it in the power of the Holy Spirit to convince non-believers and challenge and comfort believers. The prophet will have the ability to persuasively declare God's Word and will do so. Since the completion of the Canon of the Scripture the prophet receives only revelation that is in harmony with biblical revelation. He does not receive extra-biblical revelation.

Dynamic:

The person with the gift of the prophet is used of God to stir believers with God's truth. In the Scriptures the prophets were predictors as well as proclaimers. They were foretellers of the future and forthtellers in speaking God's truth. Today the predictive element has been minimized since we have the Canon of the Scriptures. Proclaiming is the primary function of the prophet.

This gift may be used in revival speaking, in exposing sin problems in a church, and in counseling to help point out sin in a person's life. This person can be a pastor when he has other gifts that give him balance suitable for that role. He also may be used in prison ministries, migrant ministries, and mission ministries.

Every gift is for evangelism! The gift of the prophet is especially powerful for sharing Christ and drawing the net. The lost need the Word of God spoken with authority and conviction as the prophet might share it. The prophet must be equipped to share Christ personally. He must develop sensitivity and a burden for the lost.

Description:

The person with the gift of the prophet usually has some and perhaps most of the following qualities:
—Very discerning
—Desires to be alone
—Strong self-image
—Not very patient with people and their problems
—More pleasant when not speaking and preaching
—Individualistic
—Opinionated
—Strong sense of duty
—Not inhibited, but expressive
—Likely to be authoritative, especially about Scripture
—Dominant, not submissive

—Burdened to expose sin
—More likely to be hostile than tolerant, especially about sin
—Less discerning than he thinks he is
—Preaches for conviction

Difficulties:

The prophet can be negative and critical. He sees problems and speaks out about them. He may have problems developing close friends. He is more likely to be depressed than light-hearted. People tend to avoid him or respond in anger if they do not repent.

Dangers:

Satan attacks and causes pride and self-righteousness that leads to anger and bitterness in the prophet. The prophet is in danger of developing a spirit of unforgiveness, a lack of compassion, and discouragement because of the unrepentant attitudes of others. He is prone to have a pessimistic attitude. His temperament makes him susceptible to fall into the sins he preaches against.

His temperament causes him not to like to study, relying on others to do his background work. He may have a poor memory for details. He over-categorizes, judges others quickly, tries to convict others rather than letting the Spirit convict, tends to be selfish, and is likely to stir up trouble. He is able to hold an audience's attention.

Delight:

The gift of the prophet is powerful within the Body of Christ. The prophet declares the Word of God with power. This enables the church to experience Spirit-filled correction and direction for revival. He helps the church focus on the high ideals of God.

Do You Think You Have the Gift of the Prophet?

On a scale of one to 10, with one being least and 10 being greatest, respond to the following questions:

_____ To what extent do you think you have the gift of the prophet?

_____ To what extent are you exercising this gift as you follow Christ?

List the ways you are practicing the use of the gift of the prophet.

_____

_____

_____

List the ways you believe God wants you to exercise the gift of the prophet.

_____

_____

_____

GIFT OF THE EVANGELIST

Definition:

The gift of the evangelist provides special ability to communicate the message of Christ's saving gospel to non-believers in such a way that they respond by receiving Christ, becoming His disciples, and becoming responsible members of the Body of Christ. The evangelist has the special ability to motivate and equip believers to share Christ with non-believers.

Dynamic:

The gift of the evangelist provides leadership in the church for reaching the lost for Christ. This gift is used to help members of the Body develop a burden for souls and to help the corporate Body develop a climate of evangelistic concern. The evangelist is used by God to motivate and equip believers for personal witnessing and soul-winning.

The gift of the evangelist is used in the local church to develop and encourage outreach visitation and programs for personal witnessing. The evangelist is used by God to preach the gospel in crusades and revivals with a special anointing for drawing the net and leading people to commitment to Christ. The evangelist is used in special evangelistic events, church planting, altar calls, and invitations to call the lost to Christ.

Members of the Body with the gift of the evangelist continue to help the church grow in vitality by reaching new converts who bring the freshness of enthusiasm for Christ and a renewed passion for reaching the lost.

Every gift is for evangelism! Especially the gift of the evangelist enables the person with that gift to effectively witness for Christ and lead the lost to Him. The evangelist must have a burden to reach the lost and to equip other believers to share Christ.

Description:

The evangelist is usually outgoing, active socially, jovial, well groomed, and neatly dressed. He communicates well, is compassionate toward people and understanding of them, and is sympathetic toward sinners. The evangelist enjoys being the center of attention. He usually displays the qualities of enthusiasm, impulsiveness, a lack of discipline, decision-making on the basis of emotions, and being talkative to the point of often interrupting others. He tends to believe strongly in "confrontational evangelism."

Difficulties:

The evangelist has difficulties within himself and from the attitudes of others. Within himself he may face struggles with sincerity and integrity. He thinks everyone should be involved in evangelism. Sometimes he may turn people off by pressing for a decision and thinks every message should be an attempt to win the lost. He tends to dominate people.

Difficulties from others include their feeling that because he emphasizes evangelism, he is weak on teaching the entire Scriptures. Some believe he is not interested in other church programs. Others may think he is more interested in numbers than people and that he judges spirituality by the number of people won to Christ. Some think he is pushy.

Dangers:

One of the grave dangers to the church regarding the gift of the evangelist is an erroneous teaching about evangelism. Some have estimated that from five to 10 percent of the membership of a church will have the gift of "evangelism" and that they are the ones who are to do the witnessing in the church. This is not only non-scriptural; it is anti-biblical.

The reality is that there is no "gift of evangelism." The gift is that of the "evangelist." Those who have the gift of the evangelist are not assigned to do all the witnessing. They are especially gifted to reach the lost for Christ and to equip others to reach them. But, every believer has the assignment of witnessing for Christ. Some believers and even leaders use the fact that they do not have the gift of the evangelist as a cop-out from witnessing. No believer should seek to find an excuse not to witness. As all members of the Body use their gifts to share Christ and to enhance the witness of the church, the fullness of joy comes to both. The church will be alive and growing.

Dangers to the evangelist are many. Satan attacks the evangelist in subtle ways to bring defeat. He does not want the evangelist to be successful in winning souls to Christ. He attacks with temptations of discouragement when the numbers of converts are few. When the number of converts is large, the evangelist is tempted toward pride. He may see people as numbers rather than people with needs. Sometimes the evangelist becomes so caught up in evangelism, he neglects the disciplines for spiritual growth. Subsequently his own spiritual growth is arrested. The evangelist is subject to temptations to manipulate and use people, to a lack of integrity about money and methods, and to sensationalism.

Delight:

The gift of the evangelist helps the church grow in number and in maturity. The evangelist is gifted to help the church harvest souls for Christ. He encourages and equips believers to share Christ effectively with the lost.

Do You Think You Have the Gift of the Evangelist?

On a scale of one to 10, with one being least and 10 being greatest, respond to the following questions:

_____ To what extent do you think you have the gift of the Evangelist?

_____ To what extent are you exercising this gift as you follow Christ?

List the ways you are practicing the use of the gift of the Evangelist.

_____

_____

_____

List the ways you believe God wants you to exercise the gift of the Evangelist.

_____

_____

_____

THE GIFT OF THE PASTOR

Definition:

The gift of the pastor provides the God-given ability to be a shepherd of the flock and to feed, nurture, and care for the people of God. The term shepherd and pastor are used interchangeably. The term "pastor" is used for the leader of the church (Acts 20:28). The pastor is leader, administrator, preacher, role model, and shepherd of the church. Usually when a person is an effective pastor, he possesses other gifts, especially the gifts of speaking, administration, and others. Many others in the church have the pastoral gift to assist in shepherding and giving pastoral care to the people of God.

Dynamic:

The gift of the pastor provides spiritual leadership to move the church forward on mission for Christ as he oversees the work. As a pastor-shepherd, he leads, feeds, guards, protects, and oversees the flock. He is the "player-coach, leader" of the team. He is the shepherd who cares for his sheep under the Chief Shepherd, Jesus, our Lord.

The pastor is an equipper of the people of God. He equips the members of the church to do their work of ministry for the building up of the Body of Christ. He multiplies himself as he equips and involves others in ministry and witness. As the church reaches people for Christ, their needs for nurture and spiritual guidance must be met. One pastor cannot shepherd all the people. Meeting the needs of all the people requires the ministry of the laity as well as the pastor. Pastors must train the people and equip them to shepherd one another. This enables the church to abundantly grow as the needs of the people are met. They are strengthened and enabled to care, witness, and minister to others.

Others in the church as well as the senior pastor have the gift of the pastor. The pastoral gift may be used as pastor or assistant pastor, Sunday School teacher, bus pastor, cell-group leader. institutional leader, nursing-home ministry, scout troop leader, and special group leader (youth, children, singles). Every member can assist in providing caring pastoral ministry to other members and to non-members in the community.

Every gift is for evangelism! The gift of pastor is especially effective in witnessing for Christ. Every pastor must have a burden for the lost and be equipped to intentionally witness to them. He must equip the members of the Body to share Christ.

Description:

The pastor is usually a patient, caring, people-centered person. He has a pleasing personality that tends to draw people to him. He is an expressive, composed, and sensitive leader who serves with authority. He has a burden to see people grow and is willing to study and prepare to feed his flock. He is more relationship oriented than task oriented. He has compassion and is tolerant of people's weaknesses. He can do many things well.

Difficulties:

Others often think it is the pastor's job to do all the work of the church and at the same time to be always available. They think he knows all the answers. Many think it is his job to do all the evangelism, but he may become so consumed with his pastoral duties that he becomes unevangelistic. He may become so overly involved in trying to do everything himself that he does not grow and, thus, burns out himself.

Dangers:

When the pastor does not equip the people and does not delegate work to be done, his load will become too heavy because he tries to do it all. Satan tempts him to become proud and puffed up because the people look up to him. If he does not delegate and share the workload, he becomes subject to burnout. Sometimes family problems develop because the pastor is too busy, spends too little time with his family, and gives them too little attention.

Delight:

The gift of pastor is the key to the health and growth of the church. A church will reflect the leadership of its pastor.

Do You Think You Have the Gift of the Pastor?

On a scale of one to 10, with one being least and 10 being greatest respond to the following questions.

_____ To what extent do you think you have the gift of the pastor?

_____ To what extent are you exercising this gift as you follow Christ?

List the ways you are practicing the use of the gift of the pastor.

_____

_____

_____

List the ways you believe God wants you to exercise the gift of the pastor.

_____

_____

_____

THE GIFT OF THE TEACHER

Definition:

The gift of the teacher provides the special, God-given ability to assimilate, organize, and communicate truth that will encourage and equip believers for witness and ministry and contribute to the health and growth of the Body of Christ.

Dynamic:

The God-anointed teacher will communicate knowledge of the truth of the Word of God with clarity, accuracy, and simplicity. This ministry helps to build strength, stability, and servanthood into the life of the Body needed to carry out the mission of Christ. The teacher spoken of in Ephesians 4:11 is an equipper of others, even other teachers. This teacher is the "*didaskalos*" (Greek for master or teacher). This person is a scholar who learns and teaches with more depth than others in the church. The challenge is to teach the great biblical doctrines and truth and handle interpretation problems with such simplicity that a seventh-grade child and those of limited educational training can understand.

God places many teachers in the church. They will be of varied personalities, temperaments, and degrees of giftedness to be able to teach every age group in the church. He combines the gift of teaching with other gifts to enable the teacher to lead a group or Bible class to reach people and disciple them. Some who do not appear to have the gift of the teacher actually do. They may be able to help others in discovering God's great truths without lectures or formal presentations but through guiding them in learning.

One church did a gift inventory with its members filling out the forms. At the conclusion a very quiet and gracious man who had started a Sunday School class and had seen it grow tremendously went to his pastor. He said, "I feel I must resign. The gift inventory showed that I do not have the gift to teach. I do not want to stand in the way. You need to get someone who has the gift of teaching." The pastor replied, "You have grown one of our best classes. You are a good teacher. You must keep on teaching and doing what you have been doing." Not everyone fits the same mold! God enables believers to teach and train others through different techniques and methods. A true teacher has a passion that will find a way to get the truth through to hearts and minds. The church is blessed that recognizes and utilizes the diversity of teaching abilities of its members.

The gift of the teacher may be used to teach in a local church Sunday School or as a Bible Institute teacher. It may be used in developing curriculum, writing literature, teaching teachers, and correspondence instruction. The gifted teacher may serve in a church, college, or seminary, or on the mission field.

Every gift is for evangelism! The gift of the teacher is a powerful gift to be used in personal witnessing. The teacher can instruct the non-believer in the faith of Christ and guide him through the conversion experience. The teacher needs to be equipped to share Christ and develop a burden for the lost. Teachers are to equip other believers by teaching them how to share Christ effectively.

Description:

The believers with the spiritual gift of the teacher have a deep love for the Word of God with a burden to know and teach it. They are usually somewhat introverted and self-disciplined and enjoy reading and studying. They prefer teaching groups rather than individuals and enjoy using charts, graphs, and lists. They are sometimes technical and usually methodical. They are thinkers who like it quiet. They teach with enthusiasm that stimulates others to learn. Teachers are usually objective in decision making.

Difficulties:

The perception others have of teachers is that they sometimes give too many details. They sometimes think the teacher is more interested in presenting facts than in the students. Sometimes teachers become so caught up in their material that they become boring to the hearers.

Dangers:

Teachers are in danger of developing pride and a feeling of superiority because of their knowledge. This is often reinforced by the affirmation of their authority by others. Teachers may become so absorbed with the material they are studying and presenting that they lose sight of people's need. When others become disinterested, the teacher may become discouraged and lose enthusiasm for teaching.

Delight:

The gift of the teacher is a delight to the Body of Christ. It enables the members to be equipped for living, witnessing, and ministering.

Do You Think You Have the Gift of the Teacher?

On a scale of one to 10, with one being least and 10 being greatest, respond to the following questions:

_____ To what extent do you think you have the gift of the teacher?

_____ To what extent are you exercising this gift as you follow Christ?

List the ways you are practicing the use of the gift of the teacher.

_____

_____

_____

List the ways you believe God wants you to exercise the gift of the teacher.

_____

_____

_____

ENABLING GIFTS

The enabling gifts provide the special ability to give support to the ministry of the Body of Christ. The four enabling gifts are faith, discernment, wisdom, and knowledge. They instill the qualities needed for effectiveness in growth and ministry into the lives of individuals and into the life of the Body. They are catalytic in their use of helping stimulate and empower the use of other gifts. Believers and churches can encourage the development and use of the enabling gifts.

THE GIFT OF FAITH

Definition:

The gift of faith is the supernatural ability to believe God and to cooperate with Him in His mighty works.

Dynamic:

The Bible speaks of several levels of faith. It speaks of saving faith, living faith, and the spiritual gift of faith. Each has the same basis—our gracious, trustworthy God. The foundation of the entire Body of Christ is faith in our living Lord. Every believer has faith, *saving faith*. We are saved "by grace . . . through faith" (Eph. 2:8-9). There is no other way to be saved.

Every believer has *living faith*. "The just shall live by faith" (Hab. 2:4). Paul quoted this verse in Romans 1:17 and in Galatians 3:11. It was quoted by the writer of Hebrews in Hebrews 10:38, who then said, "Without faith it is impossible to please Him" (Heb. 11:6). The Father has given each person a "measure of faith" (Rom. 12:3). Our faith is to be grown or developed. It can be increased. As our faith is stretched and put to the test, it increases.

The *gift of faith* is another dimension in the spiritual life of a believer and in the Body of Christ. It is associated with the miraculous. This is the special gift to believe God for His mighty works in accomplishing supernaturally what could not be done through human agency. It charges the church with energy and expectation because it lifts the confidence of the Body from the level of human dependence to dependence on what God can do. As the gift of faith is exercised, the church begins to operate out of God's resources. This is liberating for believers individually and for the church corporately. The use of the gift of faith lifts the church to a higher plain of life and ministry.

Every gift is for evangelism! The gift of faith is especially powerful in helping a believer to share Christ effectively. This gift enables a believer to pray for the lost and by faith claim them for Christ. Those who have the gift of faith need to be equipped to intentionally share Christ and to have a burden for the lost.

Description:

The believers who have the gift of faith will have vision that others do not have. They will believe God for the supplying of needs in a supernatural way. When the situation is dark and hope has faded from many, they will trust God for the impossible with an unshakable conviction that He will bring it to pass. Those with the gift of faith have been the catalysts for the progress of the church through the centuries. The church is built up, the lost reached for Christ, and the faith of believers encouraged by the exercise of the gift of faith in the Body.

Almost every time the gift of faith is mentioned or written about the great nineteenth-century saint, George Muller, is referred to. Through his gift of faith God supplied the needs of his orphanage that took care of 2,000 orphans in Bristol, England. He never made public appeals but simply believed God for the supply of millions of dollars in money and provisions.

Another great man of faith was Manley Beasley, who died just after the collapse of the Berlin Wall and the Communist rule in the Soviet Union. I asked Manley to lead our church in a conference on prayer and faith. He focused on the promise of Philippians 1:6, "Being confident of this very thing, that He who has begun a good work in you will complete it until the day of Jesus Christ." His theme was "What God Initiates, God Completes!"

In private conversation Manley invited me to go Switzerland the next year to speak at a conference on "Revival" for pastors from Eastern European countries. He said, "God has told me He is going to give revival in Eastern Europe during my lifetime!"

I found it exciting to think about being involved in such a conference. But, we were relocating our church facility and the work was very demanding. I regretfully declined. But, I thought, "Manley, are you sure God told you this? You are in terrible health and could die any time. It is not apparent that God is doing anything to bring revival in Eastern Europe!" (Manley had already been near death many times and was at that time having to use dialysis treatments to survive.)

Can you guess what happened a short while before Manley died? The Berlin Wall came crashing down! Communism fell in the Soviet Union! The Romanian dictator was assassinated. And revival broke out! Billy Graham had conducted crusades in Eastern European countries. Otherwise, no other predictable evidence existed that such a revival would happen! But, Manley Beasley knew by faith what God would do, and he was preparing for His mighty work. Our God is able!

People who have the gift of faith usually have a vision for the future. They are goal-oriented, possibility-thinkers. Believers with this gift have altered the course of history. God has used them for great advances for the Body of Christ.

Difficulties:

The difficulties for those with the gift of faith are the heartbreaks of being misunderstood by others in the Body. They are sometimes called unrealistic because no concrete evidence exists that what they believe is going to happen will happen other than believing God for it. They are branded as impractical risk-takers. It is difficult for those who truly have a gift of faith, because so many charlatans profess that gift and deceive many who ultimately become disappointed and disillusioned. They then find it difficult to accept the person with the genuine gift of faith.

Dangers:

Satan can use the negativism of others toward the person with the gift of faith within the church to create disunity and dysfunctionality. The person who has the gift may be emotionally injured to the extent he distances himself from the Body. Then his gift will not be effectively used in building up the Body. False teachers often use the claim of the gift of faith to deceive many. Many counterfeiters prey on immature believers in this way.

Delight:

The church is greatly blessed by members with the gift of faith. They help others get the vision God has given for the church. They encourage others in obeying God rather than settling for what seems humanly possible. Those with the gift of faith have been responsible for much of the advancement of the work of God throughout history.

Do You Have the Gift of Faith?

On a scale of one to 10, with one being least and 10 being greatest, respond to the following questions:

_____ To what extent do you have the gift of faith?

_____ To what extent are you exercising this gift as you follow Christ?

List the ways you are practicing the use of the gift of faith.

_____
_____
_____

List the ways you believe God wants you to exercise the gift of faith.

_____
_____
_____

THE GIFT OF DISCERNMENT

Definition:

The gift of discernment is the God-given ability to distinguish right from wrong, truth from error, and to evaluate situations, attitudes, and the spirit of persons based on God's Word.

Dynamic:

The gift of discernment is a great asset to the Body of Christ. Those who have been given this gift enable the church to distinguish between truth and falsehood. They help protect the church from false pastors, prophets, and teachers. The church is stabilized and strengthened through the use of this gift in training other members in sound biblical doctrine. Immature and shallow members are easy prey for cults and false religions. They devise plans to deceive unsuspecting believers and lead them into their heretical movements. Leaders and members with the gift of discernment help the church equip believers not only to withstand the onslaught of heresies but to know how to counteract their teachings and evangelize them.

Every gift is for evangelism! The gift of discernment enables believers to understand the needs of the lost and how to share Christ at the point of their need. Those with this gift need to be equipped to share Christ and led to have a burden for those who are lost.

Description:

Those who have the gift of discerning of spirits can sense it when deception is being used and truth is forsaken. Combined with other gifts such as administration and pastor, it enables a pastor to be highly effective in leading a church. It is a quality that prepares a believer to be a very effective counselor. The gift of discerning of spirits can be used to help other believers develop the ability to discern.

A banker was asked how bank employees were trained to detect counterfeit money. He was asked if they were taught characteristics of the counterfeit. His reply was, "No, we send the clerks to the Federal Reserve Bank to count money. They spend two weeks doing nothing but counting money. The problem with counterfeit money is not the ink but the paper. Our clerks handle the money. They handle the real thing so much that when a counterfeit goes through their hands, they can pull it out without even looking down." You learn discernment by learning the real thing. Knowing Christ and His truth equips believers to distinguish between the true and the false.

Difficulties:

The difficulties for those who have the gift of discernment of spirits are both internal and external. When they drift from Christ, become carnal, and self-centered, their gift becomes a burden and source of sadness for them. They are able to discern problems and detect inconsistencies in the lives of people. When they are not walking in the Spirit, instead of ministering to people and edifying the church, they grow bitter, resentful, and depressed. Sometimes they become so disillusioned that they drop out of church altogether. Another difficulty is misperception. They may misinterpret attitudes, behavior, and speech. They may become critical, attacking, and confrontational toward others.

Externally, others may begin to avoid those who have a gift of discerning of spirits. Some people will feel intimidated and find it difficult to be around them. When they become confrontational, some will be antagonistic toward them. The life of a person with this gift can be a lonely one.

Dangers:

The critical danger for the person with the gift of discerning of spirits is to cease to walk in the Spirit and allow Satan to use them to create hostility and confusion. As the person becomes critical and attacking, it infects the Body of Christ with anger and disunity. The Body of Christ can be built up or torn down by the use of the gift of discernment of spirits.

Delight:

The church is greatly blessed when the gift of discernment is present in its membership. It is a tremendous asset in the securing of a pastor and other ministers on its staff. It helps in utilizing lay leadership and in planning major projects. Members with this wonderful gift assist one another in resolving problems and following God's plans for their lives.

Do You Have the Gift of Discernment?

On a scale of one to 10, with one being least and 10 being greatest, respond to the following questions.

_____ To what extent do you think you have the gift of discernment?

_____ To what extent are you exercising this gift as you follow Christ?

List the ways you are practicing the use of the gift of discernment.

_____

_____

_____

List the ways you believe God wants you to exercise the gift of discernment:

_____

_____

_____

THE GIFT OF WISDOM

Definition:

The spiritual gift of wisdom is the God-given ability to understand and apply knowledge to meet specific needs in Christ's Body.

Dynamic:

The spiritual gift of wisdom can be used greatly in the Body of Christ to help individual believers and the church to understand God's perspective on life situations and share those insights in a simple, understandable way. This gift provides the ability to explain what to do and how to do it. When leaders possess this gift and use it in developing the church, it can help avoid many pitfalls and experience healthy growth. The gift of wisdom will help the church adequately plan for evangelism, ministry, and growth.

Description:

The gift of wisdom is an enabling gift that can be used in the Body to help develop wisdom in the lives of all the members. Each believer has a measure of wisdom. Their wisdom can grow if it is exercised. The Father promised, "If any of you lacks wisdom, let him ask of God, who gives to all liberally and without reproach, and it will be given to him. But let him ask in faith, with no doubting, for he who doubts is like a wave of the sea driven and tossed by the wind" (James 1:5-6). Wisdom is increased through the "testing of your faith", according to James 1:3.

Every gift is for evangelism! The gift of wisdom especially enables a believer to share Jesus effectively because he or she can discern how to approach different people with the gospel. Every believer needs to be equipped for intentional witnessing and have a burden for the lost.

Difficulties:

Those who have the gift of wisdom have an understanding that others do not possess. They face the difficulty of dealing with their own emotions as they are affected by the decisions of those who have less wisdom. If they do not walk in the Spirit and do not produce the fruit of the Spirit, the unwise decisions of others can be difficult for them. They may become angry, discouraged, and defeated. When the church and/or its leadership make unwise decisions, they may be disillusioned, become discouraged and even drop out of church.

Dangers:

A danger of the gift of wisdom is disruption of the fellowship and unity of the church. Conflict can arise when those who have the gift of wisdom surface issues that others do not want to face. The person with the gift of wisdom faces the danger of becoming impatient and angry when unwise decisions are made.

Delight:

The gift of wisdom enables the Body to function effectively with spiritual maturity. Members learn to apply their knowledge righteously and effectively to carry out the commission of Christ.

Do You Have the Gift of Wisdom?

On a scale of one to 10, with one being least and 10 being greatest, respond to the following questions:

_____ To what extent do you think you have the gift of wisdom?

_____To what extent are you exercising this gift as you follow Christ?

List the ways you are practicing the use of the gift of wisdom.

_____
_____
_____

List the ways you believe God wants you to exercise the gift of wisdom.

_____
_____
_____

THE GIFT OF KNOWLEDGE

Definition:

The spiritual gift of knowledge is the God-given ability to know and understand information that is not apparent to others.

Dynamic:

The gift of knowledge is vital to the Body of Christ. It enables individual believers to discover and collect information that is valuable to the church for its planning and decision-making. They are able to analyze and organize large amounts of information and provide it when necessary. This gift enables believers to grasp significant Scriptural ideas and truths and mold them into constructive ways about growth in the Body of Christ. Often those who have this gift are attracted to the ministry of teaching in our colleges and seminaries. But, this gift is greatly needed in the Bible-teaching ministry of local churches. Christians need an investigative approach to the study of God's Word. As the Word is shared creatively concerning our relationship to individuals, institutions, and society, our ability as Christians to make a difference will be greatly enhanced. As the gift of knowledge is used in the Body, all members better understand their mission and how to accomplish it.

Every gift is for evangelism! The gift of knowledge enables a believer to know how to approach the lost and share information they need to come to know Christ. They must be equipped to use their knowledge to intentionally share the gospel of Christ with those who need Him. They need to be led to have a burden for the lost.

Description:

The gift of knowledge is an enabling gift. It is a catalyst for the equipping of the members of the Body. Those who have the gift of knowledge find joy in discovering the reasons and purposes behind what has happened as well as the occurrence itself. They are usually studious and private, giving themselves to in-depth research. They are often more comfortable with ideas than with people.

Difficulties:

The activism in modern society causes it to be increasingly difficult for those who possess the gift of knowledge to pursue it with excellence. It takes time for study and research that is sometimes not permitted for church leaders today. The result is often shallowness in biblical understanding and doctrine.

This is a gift that is easy for both individual believers and churches to neglect. Others, especially immature believers, sometimes avoid the person with this gift due to their own feelings of inferiority. Some believers who have the gift of knowledge are not capable of effective communication. They find it difficult to present their knowledge in an interesting way. They get caught up in facts, details, and minutia and become boring to others.

Dangers:

The grave danger for the church occurs when the spiritual gift of knowledge is ignored or neglected and the church becomes biblically and theologically shallow. The trends toward "feel-good religion" and subjective, experiential theology makes the communication of the knowledge of truth unpopular. When pastors are not adequately trained doctrinally and theologically, they do not realize the value of the ministry of those with the gift of knowledge. Therefore, they sometimes lead the church to avoid emphasizing this gift.

Delight:

The gift of knowledge is a fabulous blessing to the church. Members with this gift minister and witness effectively because they understand God's truth.

Do You Have the Gift of Knowledge?

On a scale of one to 10, with one being least and 10, being greatest, respond to the following questions.

_____ To what extent do you think you have the gift of knowledge?

_____To what extent are you exercising this gift as you follow Christ?

List the ways you are practicing the use of the gift of knowledge.

_____

_____

_____

List the ways you believe God wants you to exercise the gift of knowledge.

_____
_____
_____

ACTIVITIES

List the five "equipping gifts."
1. _____
2. _____
3. _____
4. _____
5. _____

List the four "enabling gifts."
1. _____
2. _____
3. _____
4. _____

Why are these nine gifts called support gifts?

_____
_____
_____

How can the enabling gifts combine with other gifts to benefit the Body?

_____
_____
_____

Chapter Seven

Service Gifts
Get the Job Done
Outline

The six service gifts are listed in this chapter. They are the gifts of ministry, exhortation, administration/leadership, mercy, giving, and hospitality. Each is discussed under the following outline:

Definition
Dynamic
Description
Difficulties
Dangers
Delight

Chapter Seven

Service Gifts
Get the Job Done

Service gifts provide a way for the church to do its work. The majority of the members of a church have one or more of these gifts to some extent. Service gifts are task-oriented. They are used to care for multitudes of details in the operation of the corporate Body and to care for people. There are six service gifts. They are the gifts of ministry (service, helps), exhortation, administration (leadership), mercy, giving, and hospitality. All of these gifts are to be used in witness for Christ. They help the Body of Christ reach different people in different ways.

The service gifts give practical application to the faith of the Lord Jesus Christ. They combine with the other gifts to help make up a fully equipped Body. Together they form a powerful team to fulfill the mission and ministry of the church. Let's place each under the microscope of close examination to understand how they can be identified and used.

THE GIFT OF MINISTRY

Definition:

The gift of ministry is the God-given ability to recognize and meet needs, to serve, and to help by taking the initiative to give practical assistance with no thought of recognition. It enables believers to serve Christ, the church, and individual people.

136

Dynamic:

The gift of ministry is vitally important to the Body of Christ. Those who have this gift enhance the life and work of the church in two major ways. They are able to perceive needs and opportunities in the lives of people and of the church. They have a God-given ability to give practical assistance to meet these needs and help individuals and the church to move forward on the mission of Christ. Their use of the gift of ministry encourages others to give themselves unselfishly in ministry to others. They help to influence the entire church to develop a spirit of love and caring ministry to others. Caring ministry enhances evangelistic outreach powerfully.

Three major words are used in the New Testament to convey the fullness of this gift. They are ministering, serving, and helping. The Greek word *diakonia* in Romans 12:7 is translated "ministry." It is the word from which the term deacon comes. It is the term Jesus used as a mark of true discipleship. In Acts 6 it was used for "serving tables." It came to mean to "help, serve, care for, support, and aid." Another Greek word is *antilempsis* in 1 Corinthians 12:28, translated "helps." Its meaning is to help, support, undergird, and aid.

The gift of ministry practically supports every area of the life and work of a church. This gift permeates the Body of Christ when it is spiritually healthy. God intends for every believer to share in ministry to build up the Body (Eph. 4:12). Ministry is a near universal gift among believers. Every believer can minister to some extent. Some believers have the gift of ministry as their primary gift. They both minister and encourage as well as equip others for ministry. But, every Christian is a minister. There is a way each member can participate in the ministry and growth of the church.

Every gift is for evangelism! God uses those with the gift of ministry in a wonderful way to reach the lost for Christ. There is no better way to open the door for a personal witness for Christ than through caring ministry. They need to be equipped to intentionally share Christ and to lead the lost to Him.

Description:

Believers with the gift of ministry are motivated to help others and free them so they can use their gift effectively. They are ready and willing to pitch in and serve anywhere with a joyful spirit. They place themselves under others and at their disposal. They have a spirit of humility and love for Christ and for people. They serve in the background and want to avoid recognition but are indispensable to the Body. They are always ready to serve. Their chief ability is their availability.

People who have the gift of ministry often focus on projects. They are usually task-oriented and always ready to take care of even the most mundane details that help get the essentials done. They contribute much to the smooth functioning of the church both in its organization and in meeting needs. In the Scriptures these people are referred to as servants. Their servant spirit is refreshing and inspiring to the church. Their service is like oil to the machinery of the church.

One of the finest illustrations of a person with the gift of ministering I have known was Clint Harpster, a man of about 60 years. He had been a nominal church member for years but came to a new and deeper commitment of his life to Christ. As pastor, I had preached and led the church to realize that every believer is a minister and a witness. Clint had never thought he could do anything to serve His Lord. The Holy Spirit stirred his spirit to find what God wanted him to do to serve our Lord. He came to me and said, "Pastor, I have been a member of this church for many years. I have never been asked to do anything for my Lord and my church. But, I want to do something. I think I have found something I can do. I have noticed that the church buses are dirty. It would be much better to have clean buses to pick up people to help reach them for Christ. Would it be all right for me to wash and clean them every Saturday morning?"

Clint did exactly that. Soon he found other ways he could serve. Before long he started making visits with the bus captains and helped them minister to people. He came to realize that many of the people they visited had special needs. Some needs were physical, but many were spiritual. Their needs broke his heart. He began to find ways to help them with their needs. Clint participated in witness training and started sharing Christ with them personally. One after another received Christ and followed Him. What had begun as a desire to simply meet a need for people to have a clean bus to ride in resulted in the greatest ministry that can be done. Clint helped people come to know Jesus Christ and follow Him. God used him as a soul-winner.

The gift of ministry can be used in many ways in the work of our Lord. Some of those ways are:

1. Helping older people with jobs around their homes that they are no longer capable of doing.

2. Helping with children through church programs, caring for them in the community, teaching them the Word of God, seeking to reach them for Christ, discipling them, and reaching their families for Christ.

3. Helping in the details of the church organization, from secretarial work to benevolence ministries to outreach activities.

4. Helping in the family ministry and the watch-care of church members.

5. Helping meet needs of single women and widows through assistance with their cars, home repairs, etc. Helping meet physical, emotional, social, and spiritual needs of singles.

6. Helping with baking and preparing meals for those who are bereaved, for newcomers, for mission centers, and for the homeless.

7. Helping in many and varied mission projects.

Difficulties:

The difficulties faced by those with the gift of ministry include rising expectations of others. They are so willing to serve that they try to respond to every need. Others, then, continue to refer more and more needs for ministry to them until the load becomes too great. Accompanying the unrealistic expectations of others toward them is the difficulty they have of establishing limits for themselves. They need to prioritize their involvement in ministry, but they want to do everything.

Dangers:

Two major dangers lurk in the shadows for people who have the gift of ministry. One is the tendency to drift into ministering for the sake of ministering. Ministry is so enjoyable to these people and they discern needs so intensely that they often become obsessed with ministry itself. They can come to the point of simply ministering for the sake of ministry rather than to fulfill the mission of Christ in using ministry to evangelize, disciple, and edify. It is the tendency of ministries to drift away from their original purposes. Churches often start ministries for the purpose of reaching lost people and discipling them. Then, after a while, the focus subtly and unintentionally changes and begins to be placed on the ministry itself instead of its purpose.

In an earlier pastorate my wife, my wife, Kathy, and I had helped start a church located near an U.S. Air Force base. Many Air Force personnel and employees were open to the gospel and to the church, but we needed some way to reach them. We did not have access to go on base where many of them lived. We needed to attract them to our church activities and worship. As a bridging activity, we started a day-care center. Soon many were bringing their children. The day-care center was staffed with caring, ministry-gifted church members. Our day-care workers were welcomed to the base to follow up in the homes of the children. The result was that our church led the entire area in outreach, baptisms of new converts, and church growth.

A few years passed. New and better-trained personnel were employed for the day-care center. Better equipment was purchased. Attention was given to the organization. But, the day-care committee, workers, and the church lost sight of the original purpose of this ministry to reach and disciple people. The church first leveled off from growth on a plateau and then began to decline. Controversy arose over the day-care center that disrupted the unity of the church. What had been a tremendous asset to the spirit and growth of the church became a liability when the ministry left its original purpose.

The second major danger is the tendency of those with the gift of ministry to become over-involved. They have a hard time saying, "No!" They want to meet every need they observe. They respond to the requests of others as well as the needs they observe. Eventually they come to overload, but they feel guilty for not continuing to try to meet all needs. Discouragement and disillusionment follows. They face the dreaded experience of burn-out.

Delight:

The gift of ministry is a delight to the Body of Christ. It insures that the needs within the membership will be met and the church will become a ministering Body.

Do You Have the Gift of Ministry?

On a scale of one to 10, with one being least and 10 being greatest, respond to the following questions:

_____ To what extent do you think you have the gift of ministry?

_____ To what extent are you exercising this gift as you follow Christ?

List the ways you are practicing the use of the gift of ministry.

_____

_____

_____

_____

List the ways you believe God wants you to exercise the gift of ministry.

_____

_____

_____

_____

THE GIFT OF EXHORTATION

Definition:

The gift of exhortation is the God-given ability to encourage, motivate, and stimulate people to action. This gift is sometimes called the gift of encouragement.

Dynamic:

Using this gift involves a believer in a mutual work with the Holy Spirit. The word used by Paul in Romans 12:8 for this gift is *parakaleo* means "to call along side of." It is the verb form of the noun used by Jesus in John 14 for the Holy Spirit. He called the Spirit the "Paraclete" (the Comforter).

The word takes on the meaning of being a strengthener, a comforter, and encourager. It carries with it the idea of urging, appealing to, stimulating, admonishing, imploring, and motivating. The use of this ability can motivate God's people to apply and act on biblical principles in their lives and ministries. It is the ability to challenge others and bring out the best in them.

Believers with the gift of exhortation are usually practical and objective in studying the Scriptures and approaching problems. They are able to help others find solutions to their problems. Believers with this gift greatly encourage other individual members and the general Body of Christ in fulfilling the mission of its Head. God uses encouragers like Barnabas who helped Paul get started and find acceptance within the church.

God uses those with the gift of exhortation in ministries of speaking to promote the causes of the Kingdom of God, to call believers to decisions of commitment to Christ and His work, and to call nonbelievers to receive Christ. Exhortation is a gift especially used in counseling. Those with this gift serve in counseling ministries in counseling centers, school programs, drug programs, mission centers, etc. They do well in follow-up ministries with new believers to give guidance.

Every gift is for evangelism! The gift of exhortation strongly prepares one for effective personal witnessing. Their gift to encourage others can be used powerfully to share Jesus with the lost. They must be equipped for personal witnessing. They have the ability to present the gospel in mass evangelism meetings and effectively draw the net.

Description:

Those who have the gift of exhortation have the ability to motivate others to action through practical-application preaching and teaching rather than doctrinal and deeper theological emphases. They are positive people who offer hope and encouragement to believers. They are usually talkative, bubbly, enthusiastic, and somewhat impulsive. They are objective and logical—making decisions based on a deep commitment to the will of God rather than deciding and acting on the basis of emotion.

Difficulties:

The opinions of others often make it difficult for people with the gift of exhortation. Critics feel that such people are too enthusiastic. Some accuse these people of not facing reality when situations are negative. Others may think they don't place enough emphasis on Scripture and that they over-simplify everything. Such people tend to interrupt others because of their enthusiasm, creating difficulty in personal relationships.

Dangers:

People with the gift of exhortation are vulnerable to Satan's attacks through pride over their ability to influence others. Yet when results are not apparent, they tend to become discouraged. They may lose their sensitivity to people and their needs in favor of emphasizing projects. If such people are not Spirit-led, they become carnal and may use their gifts to persuade people in wrong ways. They may become superficial and insincere.

Delight:

God uses the gift of exhortation in a fantastic way when the Holy Spirit is in control of the person's life. It is an asset to the entire Body of Christ as those with the gift of exhortation encourage others to do their best and to fulfill God's purpose.

Do You Think You Have the Gift of Exhortation?

On a scale of one to 10, with one being least and 10 being greatest, respond to the following questions.

_____ To what extent do you think you have the gift of exhortation?

_____ To what extent are you exercising this gift as you follow Christ?

List the ways you are practicing the use of the gift of exhortation.

_____

_____

_____

List the ways you believe God wants you to exercise the gift of exhortation.

_____

_____

_____

THE GIFT OF ADMINISTRATION/LEADERSHIP

Definition:

The gift of administration/leadership is the special God-given ability to recognize the gifts of others, enlist, and engage them in ministry. Those who possess this gift have the ability to organize and manage people, resources, and time for effective ministry. They have the ability to coordinate details and execute the plans of leadership.

Dynamic:

The words translated "to lead, rule, administer, and govern" are found in Romans 12:8, 1 Corinthians 12:28, and Hebrews 13:7, 17, 24. These verses give a clear picture of leadership. The power that comes from the use of this gift in the Body of Christ enables the church to move forward in ministry and growth. It is essential for the coordination and utilization of all the other gifts in the Body. Without its effective use, a church will plateau and decline. Paul encouraged the gift of leadership to be exercised "with diligence" (Rom. 12:8). Leadership is to be exercised with seriousness, timeliness, enthusiasm, and deep commitment.

Leadership is primary! The church will never exceed its leadership. The speed of the leader is the speed of the team. Holy Spirit-gifted and -empowered leaders will enable the church to fulfill its mission for Christ.

Every gift is for evangelism! God wants to use those with the gift of administration/leadership to use their gifts to reach the lost for Christ. They make especially effective personal witnesses as they are equipped to share Christ. They must be role models and leaders for the church to become a witnessing Body of Christ. People do what leaders do and what leaders lead them to do. If the people are going to witness, leaders must witness.

Description:

Those who have the gift of leadership readily accept the responsibilities of stepping out to organize, plan, and manage people and programs to achieve goals. The administrator/leader is a take-charge type of person who is able to step in and give direction and orders when needed. The church needs to place people with the gift of administration/leadership in positions of leadership. They should serve in places of responsibility such as in the jobs of pastors, deacons, committee chairpersons, team leaders, Sunday School directors, and other comparable areas. They may be leaders of projects, programs, or ministries.

Throughout history the work of God has prospered when godly leadership emerged. God's work moved forward under leaders such as Moses, Joshua, Samuel, David, Solomon, Peter, and Paul. Since Bible times God has raised up leaders such as Augustine, Luther, John Wesley, George Whitefield, George Mueller, Dwight L. Moody, and Billy Graham. God provides leaders for every generation. Leaders are people of vision and self-discipline who are highly motivated, goal oriented, and assertive. People with this gift are self-giving, are often called workaholics, and want things done right. They desire to be involved in challenging tasks. When they are finished with one, they have a burden to move on to new tasks and challenges, which they are usually already planning before completing the present one. Whenever possible they delegate but know when they can't. They are willing to risk, to attempt the impossible. They make decisions on the basis of facts, not feelings.

Difficulties:

People with the gift of leadership want to win and find facing loss very difficult. They are goal-oriented and can be insensitive to people. They may be too hurried or busy to be gracious. They may be hard to please and intolerant of mistakes. Some will think they are cold, pushy, and impatient. Leadership is often a lonely place to be.

Dangers:

People who have the gift of administration/leadership are in danger of becoming proud because of their leadership position. They can become selfish and not consider those who work with them. They detest being wrong, so they may blame others when things go wrong. They may become discouraged and frustrated when their goals are not being reached.

Delight:

When the God-appointed, God-anointed leader is in God's place, outstanding possibilities happen in the Body of Christ. Such a leader is able to unify all the members of the Body, motivate them, and lead them to fulfill great achievements for the glory of Christ.

Do You Have the Gift of the Administrator/Leader?

On a scale of one to 10, with one being least and 10 being greatest, respond to the following questions.

_____ To what extent do you think you have the gift of administrator/leader?

_____ To what extent are you exercising this gift as you follow Christ?

List the ways you are practicing the use of the gift of administrator/leader.

_____

_____

_____

List the ways you believe God wants you to exercise the gift of administrator/leader.

_____

_____

_____

_____

_____

_____

THE GIFT OF MERCY

Definition:

The gift of mercy is the God-given ability to discern needs in the lives of others, to feel compassion for them, and to provide caring support for those in distress.

Dynamic:

The person who has the gift of mercy is a balm that brings relief to suffering members. This gift is powerful in helping to heal and bring good health to individual members and to the corporate Body. Paul used the Greek term, _eleon en hilaroteti,_ translated "show mercy, with cheerfulness" (Rom. 12:8). The word for "cheerfulness" is from _hilaros_ from which we get our word _hilarious._ Paul is instructing us that we are to show mercy without grudging but to do so "hilariously." Believers who have the gift of mercy do exactly that. What a joy they are to the church! They have an empathy that causes them to feel with those who have a burden.

This gift is often coupled with the gift of ministry/service/helps so that practical activity joins with compassion in meeting the needs. The gift of mercy helps a believer become a more effective witness for Christ. Many are led to faith in Christ through their compassionate witness.

Those who have the gift of mercy are needed to permeate the life of a church to help make sure it continues to be person-centered instead of drifting into an impersonal ministry. The church needs to be a caring Body of Christ. When we are filled with the Holy Spirit, all of us will exercise a spirit of mercy toward people.

Believers with a gift of mercy are especially well-suited for ministries that require direct contact with people. They may be involved in pre-school ministries, bus ministries, hospital visitation, senior-adult work, ministries to nursing homes and shut-ins, ministries to the bereaved, benevolence, mission centers, feeding the hungry and the homeless, crisis-pregnancy ministries, psychologists, counselors, and evangelistic outreach activities.

Description:

The gift of mercy usually belongs to people who are not leaders. They are mild in personality and soft-spoken. They do not want to hurt anyone's feelings by being too strong or assertive. People love them because they always appear to be caring. They are good listeners but talk easily with people, and people easily talk with them.

The person with the gift of mercy is sympathetic and sensitive and so tends to attract those who have needs. He is non-condemning, accepting of others, and self-sacrificing.

Every gift is for evangelism! God wants to use every Christian to reach the lost for Christ. God uses those with the gift of mercy to care. Caring opens the door for sharing Christ. Mercy people need to be equipped to intentionally witness. They can be taught to become sensitive to the spiritual condition of the lost as well as feeling for their physical needs.

Difficulties:

The difficulties people face often grow out of their strengths. This is true with mercy givers. They often overextend themselves because they attract needy people who consume much time and energy. They let others use them, allows circumstances to control them, and often have low self-esteem. Because of their inability to say, "No," they are often late. They lack self-discipline and have difficulty helping others to develop the discipline to take the actions necessary to resolve the issues that cause their problems. They may be indecisive and negative. Others may think they are weak and emotional.

Dangers:

People with the gift of mercy are subject to attacks of Satan at the point of pride. They may become filled with pride because people are attracted to them. Their lack of discipline causes them to have a disregard for rules and authority. They have the danger of violating confidences if they do not walk in the Spirit.

Delight:

The Body of Christ is greatly blessed by the mercy giver. God uses this gift to bless every member.

Do You Think You Have the Gift of Mercy?

On a scale of one to 10, with one being least and 10 being greatest, respond to the following questions.

_____ To what extent do you think you have the gift of mercy?

_____ To what extent are you exercising this gift as you follow Christ?

List the ways you are practicing the use of the gift of the mercy.

_____

_____

_____

List the ways you believe God wants you to exercise the gift of mercy.

_____

_____

_____

THE GIFT OF GIVING

Definition:

The gift of giving is the God-given ability to earn money and give generously and cheerfully beyond the tithe to the right things at the right times to support God's work.

Dynamic:

In Romans 12:8, Paul says the gift of giving should be done "with liberality." It is to be done from a pure heart. Giving is a privilege and the responsibility of every believer. All Christians can develop the gift of giving to some extent by being faithful and consistent in giving. The tithe (10 percent of a person's income) belongs to God. It is holy and is to be returned to Him (Lev. 27:30; Mal. 3:8-10; Heb. 7:8). Giving begins after the tithe has been returned to God. Everyone should tithe and give above the tithe. Just as all believers are to witness and minister, all are to give for the work of the Kingdom of God.

Believers with the gift of giving greatly help to provide support for the Body of Christ. They help the church to accomplish projects over and above their regular ministries. A biblical example is Barnabas, who sold his property and gave all to meet the crisis/need of the early church described in Acts 4:36-37. He gave simply, with no strings attached. Ananias and Sapphira, also, gave, but they lied about their giving and were smitten by the Hand of the Lord and died. The fact is that the gift, no matter how large or small, is not the primary thing. The priority in giving is the motive. Giving is to be done generously and cheerfully out of hearts of love.

Description:

Persons with the gift of giving have an uncanny, creative ability to invest, earn money, and gain property. They always have a desire to give and participate in what God is doing by giving money to support His Kingdom. They are particularly interested in helping people and special projects that spread the gospel of Christ. They are usually good managers, well-organized, and private—not wanting recognition for their giving. They want to know that their gifts are used responsibly.

Givers are sensitive to the needs of others. They are often compassionate people who can be greatly used of God in evangelistic outreach. Their ability to be used in personal witnessing will depend on their being equipped to share Christ and lead people to Him. As a pastor, I had the privilege of equipping an outstanding businessman, a banker, to share Christ effectively. He told me, "Pastor, many people come to talk with me about money, but beneath this surface need is always a spiritual need. I look for opportunities to share Christ at the point of their need."

God wants to use every gift for evangelism. He can use the giver in a special way. The giver has contacts with people that many members of the church would never touch. He has influence that God can use to help many come to Christ if he is sensitive to their spiritual needs and to the leadership of the Holy Spirit.

God can use givers to serve in various management areas of the church. They may serve in the financial area of the church, on a building committee, mission teams, on an advisory council, or in the communications ministry. Often the giver is effective in directing a Sunday School department or another ministry in the church.

Difficulties:

Those with the gift of giving face the difficulty of discerning where they need to give financial support. More needs than any one person can address always exist. Sometimes others do not understand when the givers do not support them or their project. Others sometimes become jealous and accuse the giver of trying to buy a position in the church or control through giving.

Sometimes givers are offended when others do not give as they do. The giver may become disgruntled and judgmental when others fail to give. He may judge the spirituality of others by what they give or do not give.

Dangers:

Givers respond to challenge and project appeals. Many givers have been injured spiritually and sometimes totally dropped out of church when insincere, charlatan types of leaders have taken advantage of their desire to give. They are subject to being used by wrongly motivated spiritual leaders. Satan may attack the giver at the point of pride over the amount he or she gives. Givers can develop a critical spirit toward those who give little. They can develop a spirit of disunity and disrupt the fellowship when they disapprove of the ways money is spent.

Delight:

When they walk in the Spirit, God uses givers abundantly to help support the ministry of the Body of Christ. God uses them in special ways to encourage leaders and other members with the hope that God will provide for what He wants the church to do. Their example can stimulate other members to give above what they would normally give.

Do You Think You Have the Gift of Giving?

On a scale of one to 10, with one being least and 10 being greatest, respond to the following questions:

_____ To what extent do you think you have the gift of giving?

_____ To what extent are you exercising this gift as you follow Christ?

List the ways you are practicing the use of the gift of giving.

_____

_____

_____

List the ways you believe God wants you to exercise the gift of giving.

_____

_____

_____

THE GIFT OF HOSPITALITY

Definition:

The gift of hospitality is the special, God-given ability to warmly receive people, especially strangers, to help them feel welcomed and accepted in the church family.

Dynamic:

The gift of hospitality is vitally important for growing the fellowship of the church. 1 Peter 4:8-10 speaks of this gift, "And above all things have fervent love for one another, for *'love will cover a multitude of sins.'* Be hospitable to one another without grumbling. As each one has received a gift, minister it to one another, as good stewards of the manifold grace of God."

The gift of hospitality involves believers in tangible expressions of love by opening their homes to others, providing food, and helping others share in fellowship. They help people, especially newcomers and strangers, feel welcome in the meetings of the church. This is valuable to the church in keeping a warm spirit of love throughout the membership. It is especially important for new believers and new members to be received and incorporated into the fellowship.

Description:

In the early church it was important for homes to be open to strangers who were traveling. There were few inns and no hotels and motels such as we have today to provide shelter. Nor did restaurants or fast-food outlets exist to provide food for travelers. Believers with the gift of hospitality opened their homes and hearts to those who had need. Today many are homeless and in need. Multitudes of people are lonely and in need of someone to care. Those with the gift of hospitality make their homes centers of redemption where people are reached and ministered to. They help lead the church to develop ministries of hospitality to care for and provide for their needs. You find them involved in benevolence and social ministries. They often engage in and host home Bible study and prayer ministries. They may be involved in new-member assimilation classes. They can be found helping feed and shelter the homeless and needy.

Every gift is for evangelism! The gift of hospitality powerfully opens the door for witness. Believers with the gift of hospitality develop a rapport with people and build relationships that enables them to share Christ in a natural and non-threatening way. It is important that their pastors and leaders equip them well for personal witnessing.

Difficulties:

Those who have the gift of hospitality are always in danger of overextending themselves because of their compassion for those in need. They find setting boundaries for those they help to be difficult. They sometimes allow others to take advantage of them.

Dangers:

The hospitality person is in danger of burnout through helping others. Satan attacks with temptations toward resentment and bitterness when the person becomes weary and feels unappreciated.

Delight:

Those who have the gift of hospitality help the Body treat guests with gracious concern. They influence members of the Body to develop sensitivity to guests and to know how to help them be involved in the fellowship.

Do You Think You Have the Gift of Hospitality?

On a scale of one to 10, with one being least and 10 being greatest, respond to the following questions:

_____ To what extent do you think you have the gift of hospitality?

_____ To what extent are you exercising this gift as you follow Christ?

List the ways you are practicing the use of the gift of hospitality.

_____
_____
_____
_____

List the ways you believe God wants you to exercise the gift of hospitality.

_____

_____

_____

Are There Any More Gifts?

Nineteen gifts have been listed and briefly discussed. These are those that are noted in Scripture. Some add several more that may be alluded to in the Word of God. Are there others? Yes, there may be others! Or, God may give several gifts to a believer so the end result will be that the utilization of this "cluster of gifts" appears to be an additional gift.

The key to effectively using our spiritual gifts is obedience to Christ. Whatever gift is needed for us to do all that He desires us to do will be surfaced in our lives by the Holy Spirit as we obey Him.

Believers Have the Potential for Every Gift!

Because of the indwelling of Christ in each believer, the potential for any gift is latent within each of us.

Our Lord Jesus Christ is the perfect person and the possessor of every gift. He lives within us (Eph. 3:17). Since the one who lives within us possesses every gift, He can give to the believer whatever gift He chooses so that he or she can obediently and effectively minister. This is a fantastic reality that causes us to be able to shout with Paul the triumphant note of victory, "I can do all things through Christ who strengthens me" (Phil. 4:13).

ACTIVITIES

List the six service gifts.

1. _____
2. _____
3. _____
4. _____
5. _____
6. _____

What is the most nearly universal gift of all the gifts?

_____

Which of these gifts is strongest in your life?

_____

What support gift can be clustered with the gift of administration/leadership to enable it to be more effective?

_____

Chapter Eight

Using Your Gifts to Share Jesus

Outline

Gifts are used in many ways to help the Body of Christ to fulfill its mission. But to carry out the Great Commission God uses every gift for evangelism.

I. God's Power Team for Witness Acts 4:31
   - The Word of God
   - The Work of the Spirit
   - The Witness of the Believer
II. God's Gifts for Witness
   - Sign Gifts
   - Support Gifts
   - Service Gifts
III. Whatever Gifts We Have, We Can Use to Share Christ

Chapter Eight

Using Your Gifts to Share Jesus

The purpose of the Body of Christ is to glorify our Lord and carry out His commission by taking His gospel to every person in our world in this generation (Matt. 28:18-20; Acts 1:8). The heart of Christ beats for souls. "He came to seek and to save that which was lost" (Luke 19:10). He loved lost humanity so much that "He bore our sins in His own body on the tree" (1 Peter 2:24). If our hearts beat like His, they will beat for souls. As Savior and Head of the Body He has gained gifts for the building up of His Body (Eph. 4:9-12). These gifts are to be used to evangelize those who are lost, to lead them to Christ, bring them into the Body, and equip them to evangelize others.

Gifts are used in many ways to fulfill the mission of the Body of Christ. But in special ways God uses every gift for evangelism. God wants to use every believer and every gift to reach those who are lost. The Acts 1:8 strategy of Jesus applies to every local church. Each church is responsible for saturating its Jerusalem (its geographical area and area of influence) with the gospel in such a way that each person can with understanding say, "Yes or No" to the claims of Christ in his or her life.

God supplies gifts and resources so each church can reach its area with the gospel. He has a powerful team of three that He has given to every church that can saturate its area with the gospel. This unbeatable team is seen in Acts 4:31, "And when they had prayed, the place where they were assembled together was shaken; and they were all filled with the Holy Spirit, and they spoke the word of God with boldness." The result was multitudes came to know Christ as Savior and Lord, and the movement of the gospel continued to expand. The believers who spoke the Word with boldness had all the different gifts. They were all used for evangelism. This is God's intention for every church.

God's Powerful Team of Three are the Word of God, the Work of the Spirit, and the Witness of the Believer

First, The Word of God

The Word of God is Power! "For I am not ashamed of the gospel of Christ, for it is the power of God to salvation for everyone who believes, for the Jew first and also for the Greek" (Rom. 1:16). What people need in order to be saved is the Good News of Christ. Every kind of thing is being used to try to get people into the church—entertain them in, advertise them in, psychologize them in, market them in. But the one thing that will change lives is the gospel of Christ.

The Word Produces Faith. "So then faith comes by hearing, and hearing by the Word of God" (Romans 10:17). Learning about world religions and studying philosophy does not grow faith. The thing that grows faith is the Word of God.

The Word of God is Like a Sword. "For the word of God is living and powerful, and sharper than any two-edged sword, piercing even to the division of soul and spirit, and of joints and marrow, and is a discerner of the thoughts and intents of the heart" (Heb. 4:12). The Word of God probes deeper than human counsel can go. Human counsel can deal with mind or our thought processes, emotions or our feelings, and will or our decision making. The Word of God penetrates into the spirit level of our lives, which effects life change. It creates the openness for conversion.

The Word of God is Like a Fire and a Hammer. "Is not my word like a fire," says the Lord , "and like a hammer that breaks a rock in pieces?" (Jer. 23:29). It melts the coldest heart and purifies the vilest heart! Like a hammer it crushes the hardest, stony heart.

The Word of God Accomplishes His Purpose. "So shall My word be that goes forth from My mouth; It shall not return to Me void, But it shall accomplish what I please, And it shall prosper in the thing for which I sent it" (Isa. 55:11). The greatest tool the church and the individual believer have is the Word of God. It gets the job done!

Second, The Work of the Spirit

The Holy Spirit Draws Non-believers to Christ. "No one can come to Me unless the Father who sent Me draws him" (John 6:44). Soul-winning is Holy Spirit work. As Jesus is lifted up, the Spirit draws non-believers to Him (John 12:32). We cannot entice, manipulate, persuade, or force anyone to come to Christ. The Holy Spirit will use us as instruments to share the Word and guide them through the conversion experience, but only He can draw them to Him. His work in their hearts makes the difference.

The Holy Spirit Convicts and Convinces the Non-believer. For a person to come to Christ, a proper heart condition must exist—repentance from sin and faith in the Lord Jesus Christ. No matter how adept we may be in witnessing, no human can give someone else the heart condition essential for salvation. "And when He has come, He will convict the world of sin, and of righteousness, and of judgment: of sin because they do not believe in Me; of righteousness, because I go to my Father and you see Me no more; of judgment, because the ruler of this world is judged" (John 16:8-11).

When we try to convict people of sin, they become resistant and offended. This is the work of the Holy Spirit. I had witnessed to Jerry several times. He courteously, but firmly said, "No," each time. One night after he had been in our worship, I felt an impression that I needed to talk to Jerry that night. I asked a deacon we called "Doc", because he was a dentist, to go with me.

Jerry greeted us at the door, "Preacher, I am glad to see you, come on in. I have just been thinking about what you preached Sunday!"

I said, "Jerry, that is why I have come! I have come to ask you to pray with us and receive Christ."

Jerry didn't answer. He simply called his wife's name and said, "Come in here. We are going to pray with the preacher tonight!"

We fell on our knees and he prayed and asked God to forgive him and for Jesus to come into his heart and life. I asked him, "If you are receiving Christ, committing your life to Him, and you are ready to obey Him and follow Him in believer's baptism, please take my hand

and say, "I will." Joyfully, Jerry took my hand and said, "I will!" Then, he exuberantly, said, "Now, what can I do for Jesus?"

The best thing that can happen to new believers is to share their witness for Christ with someone as soon as possible. I urged him, "Jerry, you have a friend named Johnny who is about like you were. He needs Christ. You can go to see him tomorrow night, tell him what happened to you, and ask him to receive Christ, too. And, Doc will go with you. Won't you, Doc?"

Doc said, "Sure, I will!" Surely enough, the next Sunday both Jerry and Johnny came down the aisle to confess Christ. The dentist was right behind them! It was a great day!

What made the difference in Jerry? At his home that night, it was like a light came on in his heart and mind. The Holy Spirit draws non-believers to Christ and enlightens their minds so they can come to Him. "He will glorify Me, for He will take of what is Mine and declare it to you" (John 16:14).

<u>The Holy Spirit Leads Believers to Encounter Those Who Need Christ.</u> "For as many as are led by the Spirit of God, these are the sons of God" (Rom. 8:14). In Acts 8 Philip was preaching and being mightily used by God in Samaria. He was told by an angel to go south to the desert of Gaza. He went not knowing why except that God had told him to go. No one was in the desert. But, would you believe—his path crossed the path of a caravan at just the point where the treasurer of the queen of Ethiopia was in his chariot reading from Isaiah 53. This was a Divine Appointment!

Philip asked a question. This is a great way to begin a soul-winning conversation. He asked, "Do you understand what you are reading?" The Ethiopian responded, "How can I unless someone guides me?" Philip began there and led him to Jesus.

The Holy Spirit works on both ends at the same time. While He was leading Philip from Gaza to the desert, He was working in the heart and mind of the Ethiopian. The Spirit led the two together for Philip to guide him through the conversion experience. The key to reaching people for Christ is obedience to the Holy Spirit. Any believer can lead people to Christ if the believer will be sensitive to the Holy Spirit and sensitive to people.

<u>The Holy Spirit Will Give You What to Say.</u> Some believers feel that they can use their gifts in service to Christ but can never witness.

Their fear is that they won't know what to say. We do need to study and learn as much as we can about the Scriptures and how to share Christ, but we will never learn enough to know what we are going to say. In a witness encounter we have to step out in obedient faith and begin. Witnessing is a dynamic and different encounter with each person. Trusting the Holy Spirit is imperative. Jesus promised, "Do not worry about . . . what you should say. For the Holy Spirit will teach you in that very hour what you ought to say" (Luke 12:11b-12).

<u>The Holy Spirit Will Use Your Mess-Ups.</u> Some believers will say they are afraid that if they try to witness, they would mess-up. But the Holy Spirit is so wonderful that He will even use our mess-ups for His glory. He would have to, wouldn't He? Between the worst of us and the best of us, there is not enough difference to make any difference. To use any of us He would have to use us in spite of us. If we will trust Him and share Christ, we can trust Him to use us.

I have a pastor friend named James. One day on his way home from the church office, he stopped by the grocery store, where he saw a member named Sue. Sue said, "Pastor, I may need to call you sometime to come to talk to my husband. He is becoming more and more difficult. He doesn't know Christ, and now he is trying to keep me from coming to church."

The pastor graciously said, "Call me any time, Sue, and I will come." That very night past midnight the phone rang. The voice said, "Hello, Pastor, this is Sue. Can you come to our house tonight? My husband and I are having trouble."

The pastor got up and put on his clothes. He hurried over to Sue's house. When he knocked, Sue came to the door in her nightgown and robe. Her husband was sitting in his easy chair in his pajamas watching the late show on television. It was late. James got right to the point. He said, "You need to get right with God. You haven't given spiritual leadership to your family."

Sue's husband was remorseful, "You are right, Pastor, I need to get right and live for God!" He prayed with the pastor and received Christ. It was a joyful time at Sue's house at 1:00 a.m. that morning.

The next day the phone rang in the pastor's office. The voice said, "Hello, Pastor, this is Sue. When you did not come to my house last night, I talked to my husband myself, and he accepted Christ and is coming with me to church Sunday."

You guessed it! On Sunday both Sues and their husbands went down the aisle at James' church. Both of them had accepted Christ. The Holy Spirit is so wonderful! He even uses our mess-ups for His glory!

Third, the Witness of the Believer

God wants to use every believer as a witness for Christ. He has given us a life-changing experience through Christ. We have a testimony to share. He has given us the Word of God to use to guide those who need Christ. He has given us the gift of the Holy Spirit who empowers us to lead them to Him. Acts 1:8 declares that Holy Spirit power has been given for witness. His power flows directly and proportionately according to our faithfulness in witness for Christ.

God has further enabled us for effective witnessing through the spiritual gifts He has given us. Every gift can be used to enhance our witness for Christ. Every non-believer is different. A same kind of cookie-cutter approach will not work in reaching everyone. They all need someone to care for them in a special way. The variety of personalities and gifts of believers enables the church to reach all types of people.

God's Gifts Are for Witness

Spiritual gifts equip those who have them to share Christ in a unique and special way using their particular gifts. Each will be able to use his or her gift to minister the Word of God in special ways in the power of the Holy Spirit at the point of the non-believer's needs.

The Sign Gifts

The Sign Gifts were given by our Lord to substantiate the gospel.

The Gift of Miracles in biblical times was used to authenticate the claims of Christ to non-believers before the Scriptures were canonized. The mighty works of God attracted non-believers to the hearing of the gospel. They became open to the Holy Spirit and to the personal witness of those God used. Today in sin-darkened, pagan areas of our world, God does His mighty works through His witnesses to affirm their witness for Christ resulting in people being saved. The gift of miracles is for evangelism.

The Gift of Healing is a gift of compassion to relieve human suffering and to bring people to know Christ. God has given a gift and ministry of healing to believers. Sometimes He supernaturally heals without human instrumentality or the use of medicine. More often His healing is through the more natural processes of using the gift of healing through those who understand medical, emotional, psychological, and spiritual needs and how to meet them. Those who are used for the healing of others have an open door to share the gospel with them. A medical missionary in Africa was used by God both supernaturally and naturally through medical means to bring healing to many. Thousands came to faith in Christ through his witness.

The Gift of Tongues and Interpretation of Tongues was used by God through the first-century church beginning at Pentecost to communicate the gospel to people of other languages and lead them to Christ. Today He gives the supernatural ability to believers to understand languages, translate the Scriptures into other languages, and share Christ with people who speak in languages different from their own and lead them to Christ.

The Support Gifts

Support Gifts are for evangelism. They are used both to witness and lead people to Christ and to equip other believers for soul-winning.

The Gift of the Apostle is used in missions and church planting today. Both missionaries and church planters have the supernatural ability to cross cultural, racial, and other barriers to lead people to Christ and incorporate them into the life of a church they are starting. There is no way to start churches apart from evangelistic effort. It requires extensive evangelistic visitation and soul-winning for new churches to grow. Glyndon Grober was a highly gifted missionary to Brazil. Through using his spiritual gift he led thousands of Brazilians to Christ and was instrumental in starting hundreds of churches. He was a consistent witness and soul-winner.

Those Who Have the Gift of the Prophet have the supernatural ability to receive and proclaim God's message. Both publicly and personally those with the gift of the prophet can share Christ with non-believers and lead them to Christ. The prophet has a special power to confront people with God's truth in such a way that those who hear experience deep conviction for sin. Many turn to Christ as Savior and Lord as this gift is used in witnessing. One who strongly exercises the gift of the prophet speaks publicly and because of that many turn to Christ. He, also, shares Christ personally as he goes about his daily activities and individually leads people to Christ consistently. The gift of the prophet is for evangelism!

The Gift of the Evangelist naturally is for evangelism. The evangelist has the gift to publicly and privately share the gospel and lead people to Christ. The evangelist personally leads the lost to Christ and motivates and equips other members of the Body to witness.

One Sunday morning an evangelist visited our worship service. During that service, several individuals made professions of faith. At the conclusion of the worship service and invitation, I introduced the evangelist and asked him to come to the platform and share a word of greeting. He did not bring a greeting. He simply said, "I believe there are others here who need Christ. I want to ask you to come now to Him." As the evangelist gave the appeal, at least 15 others received Christ and came forward to confess Him. That evangelist had the gift of drawing the net and reaping the harvest! Not every one has the gift of the evangelist, but everyone is to witness for Christ.

The Gift of the Pastor is certainly for evangelism. Shepherding the people of God offers multitudes of opportunities to personally lead people of all ages and types to Christ. It is not easy for a pastor to be consistent in personal soul-winning. Many demands will all but consume his time and energy. He must be intentional in his personal witnessing and must schedule time to spend sharing with people who need Christ. As a pastor, I set a goal to schedule the time and give the effort every week to personally lead someone to Christ. I believe that I have no right to stand in a pulpit and preach if I am not daily obedient in personal witnessing.

The Gift of the Teacher is for evangelism! A teacher has the ability to organize thoughts and material that easily can be used to explain the gospel and lead the lost to Christ. For this to happen the teacher must take the Commission of Christ seriously and develop a burden for the lost. The teacher needs to be equipped to win souls and to be intentional in sharing Christ.

The Gift of Faith is for evangelism! The person who has the gift of faith can be greatly used to lead the lost to Christ. This person has the faith to believe God and claim lost souls for Christ. He or she needs to realize that the great purpose of Christ stated in His Commission is to reach the lost. Then, this person needs to identify those who need Him, pray for them, and seek to share Christ with them. Manley Beasley was a man of great faith. He ministered to many, helping them to find victory in Christ. But, Manley had a burden for those who were lost and exercised his faith to lead great numbers of people to Christ.

The Gift of Discernment is for evangelism! It enables a believer to understand the needs and characteristics of people. Those who have this gift can sense the need, thoughts, and qualities of living of lost people. They can use their gifts in knowing how to approach and share Christ with them. Through the use of this gift, they can be very effective in leading people to know Christ.

Karen is a young woman who has the gift of discernment. She meets people easily and immediately begins to dialogue with them. Soon she perceives their point of need and draws them out. Because she has a burden for the lost, she seeks to share Christ with them and often leads them to Christ. She realized her sister-in-law was lost and struggling. Karen was driving by her apartment one afternoon. She felt an impression from the Holy Spirit to stop and see Lori. She heeded that instinct! This was unusual. She had made it a practice to never visit Lori without calling first. When she went in, she found Lori crying and reading her Bible. Within a few minutes Karen had led Lori to Christ.

The Gift of Wisdom is for evangelism! This gift enables a believer to help the lost to deal with the situations of their lives wisely and share Christ with them at the point of their need. This is a great gift to be used for evangelism. This person can wisely take the best approaches in leading the lost to Christ.

Mr. Schmucker, a retired oil company executive, had grown into his position through his wisdom. When he retired, he spent a little more of his time on the golf course. One day he needed a partner and joined to play the course with Kyle, a younger man. By the time they had played nine holes, Mr. Schmucker had built a rapport with Kyle and had discussed many of the younger man's concerns with him. He did not miss the opportunity to share Christ with Kyle. Mr. Schmucker asked for the privilege of coming to Kyle's home to discuss their spiritual needs with him and his wife. As they visited a couple of nights later, both Kyle and his wife made their decisions for Christ. The gift of wisdom can be wonderfully used for evangelism!

The Gift of Knowledge is for evangelism! It is especially effective as it is used to share Christ and seek to lead the lost to know Him. Those who have the gift of knowledge are able to share the facts and details that lost people need to understand in order to be saved. It is important that those who have this gift realize that the Commission of Christ to reach the lost is priority for every believer. They need to develop a burden for the lost and to be sensitive to the Holy Spirit.

A seminary president with several doctorate degrees had a great ability to gather and categorize information. He had a burden for souls and commitment to the Commission of Christ that caused him to be an outstanding personal soul-winner.

The Service Gifts

Service Gifts are for evangelism. They very naturally give those who have these gifts opportunities to share Jesus with many.

The Gift of Ministry/Service/Helps is for evangelism. It is almost, if not totally, universal. Every believer can minister and serve in some ways. Ephesians 4:11-12 says the purpose of believers being equipped is "for the work of ministry." Ministry opens the door for evangelism in a powerful way. Len has the gift of ministry. He is always helping somebody with some need or helping them find the right source of having the person's need met. Time and again it results in his leading the person—and sometimes the person's family—to Christ. Every believer can minister to somebody and in the process of ministering can share the gospel of Christ with them.

The Gift of Exhortation is a gift for evangelism! This gift is powerful for evangelism! Those who have the gift of encouragement are able to help lift people out of their distress and discouragement to see their hope in Christ. George was just such a person. With his gift of exhortation he could relate to every age group of people. He could always strike up a conversation with anyone he met. He would find a way to introduce spiritual thoughts into the conversation. He would direct the conversation to Jesus Christ. He led many to Christ because he had a deep commitment to Christ and His Commission. The more God used George to lead people to Christ, the more compassion he grew to have for the lost. He came to the point of intentionally seeking a way to share Christ with everyone he met.

The Gift of Administration/Leadership is for evangelism! This gift is very effective when it is used for personal witnessing for Christ. The administrator/leader is able to organize situations and material and to lead people. The person with this gift can set up systematic ways to create opportunities to personally get the gospel to lost people. Their leadership ability helps them to effectively share the plan of salvation with people and guide them through the conversion experience.

I received John's resume when we were seeking a director of recreation for our church. When he was 14 years old, he had started young using his gift of administration as a coach of a sports team. In high school he organized adult sports leagues. After college he became the director of a 300-acre recreation park with 40 employees. When he accepted Christ, he began to use his gift to reach others for Christ. What caught my attention was that he stated his priority was to lead people to Christ. He joined our church staff and did an excellent work directing our organizations. He not only led the recreation ministry and other ministries to reach the lost, but he personally led lost people to Christ!

The Gift of Mercy is for evangelism! This gift causes the person who has it to be drawn to those in need, which includes their spiritual need. They have such a heart of compassion that lost people open up to them and receive their witness without resistance. Those with the gift of mercy need to be trained to move past the surface needs of people to their spiritual needs and seek to lead them to Christ.

Beverly took a job teaching English in a junior high school. She has the gift of mercy. She was teaching in a very difficult situation in an over-crowded classroom in a dilapidated school building. The classes of 40 to 50 students were almost unmanageable. She almost broke down because of the stress and tension in the school. She continued to pray and love the students until God gave her a break-through. One afternoon she told several of the leading trouble-makers to stay after school. As she talked to them, she began to share Christ with them. All of them said they wanted to pray and receive Christ. After they did, Beverly took the children home and told their parents about what had happened. The children began to go to church. They told other young people what had happened. Others were interested. By the end of school 30 students and several parents had accepted Christ.

After school was out, Beverly planned a party for her "kids" (those who had received Christ). Other students began to ask if they could come. She invited everybody who wanted to attend. She borrowed her church's buses and activities center for them. The night of the party, the gospel was shared, and 150 young people accepted Christ. The next year it was a different school! God had used one teacher with a gift of mercy to transform a lot of lives and an entire school.

The Gift of Giving is for evangelism! Those who have the gift of giving enjoy giving to help people and special projects. They often give to support evangelistic projects. When they give to help people, through their love God opens hearts to the gospel. Givers know how to earn money. They can counsel others in their financial concerns and open the door to share the gospel and lead them to Christ.

A big guy nicknamed Tiny had the gift of giving. He made a lot of money as an entrepreneur. He tithed and gave to his church and gave abundantly to people in need. Almost every week someone came to know Christ and followed Him in baptism through Tiny's witness.

A poor family had a special need. I visited with them. They had already made a decision for Christ and said their needs were met. They said Tiny had come by. He had given them money for their crisis and had given them the spiritual gift they needed—Jesus.

The Gift of Hospitality is for evangelism! God uses this gift extraordinarily to reach the lost for Christ. Believers with this gift have a special ability to entertain, provide for the needs of guests, serve as host or hostess, and help people feel accepted and worthwhile. Their warmth and caring attracts people including those who are lost. They have a special opportunity to use their gift to share the gospel and lead people to Christ. They need to be trained and equipped to realize the spiritual need of people and how to lead them to Christ. God will use them greatly in evangelism.

Becky lives in our neighborhood. She started a home Bible-study group. One night every week Becky prepares a lovely meal or refreshments. They have warm and wonderful fellowship studying the Word of God. Becky invites people who need fellowship and encouragement. Some of them need spiritual encouragement. Some need to come to know Christ. Through her ministry of hospitality people come to know Christ. Two couples who met at her Bible study and have followed Christ plan to be married soon.

Gifts Are Given to Allow the Body to Fulfill its Mission

All the gifts needed to provide for all the ministries and operation of a church are given by God and are in the lives of the members. These gifts supply everything needed to carry out the Commission of Christ. God wants all members to exercise their gifts in their normal use. For example the giver is to give, the mercy-shower is to do acts of mercy, and the prophet is to proclaim God's truth. But all gifts are to be used for evangelistic witness and ministering.

The danger is that believers sometimes get caught up in using their "gift" and forget that our Lord's command to witness and minister. They often do not realize that one of the purposes of their gift is to use it to reach the lost for Christ.

Cop-Outs Defeat Evangelism

Some believers use some gift they claim to have as a cop-out to keep from being involved in witnessing and soul-winning. They say, "Evangelism is just not my gift! I can do some things in the church, but I can't witness!"

The truth is they use this "cop-out" to excuse themselves from witnessing. Their attitude is based on a myth made prominent by Satan and the enemies of Christ. The myth is that evangelism is a gift and only those who have it can and are responsible to witness. As was pointed out earlier "evangelism" is not a gift. It is an assignment of every believer. Every Christian is to witness. If Satan can intimidate us or convince us not to witness, he has the lost his grip. All it takes for the lost to remain lost and go to hell is for believers to remain silent about Jesus.

Our Lord commands us to witness! We have no alternative! We either obey Him in witnessing to others or live in disobedience to His command and commission.

God has wonderfully supplied for us all we need to witness for Christ and to be soul-winners! Whatever gifts we have, we can use to share Christ with those who need Him.

ACTIVITIES

What is the rationale for saying, "Every gift is for evangelism"?

_____

_____

_____

Name the three who are on God' power team for evangelism.
1. _____
2. _____
3. _____

How can the gift of faith be used for evangelism?

_____

_____

_____

What gifts do you think are in your life? How can you use them for evangelism?

_____

_____

_____

For further help in learning how to use your gifts to share Christ in a non-threatening way study my material *People Sharing Jesus*, published by Thomas Nelson Publishing Company.

Chapter Nine

Discovering and Using Your Gifts with Love
Outline

Obedience to Christ Is the Key to Knowing and Using
Spiritual Gifts

I. How Are Believers Treating Their Gifts?
- Some Are Unaware of Gifts
- Some Are Withholding Their Gifts
- Some Are Misusing Their Gifts
- Some Are Discovering Their Gifts
- Some Are Developing Their Gifts
- Some Are Dynamically Using Their Gifts

II. How You Can Discover Your Gifts
- Pray for God's Direction for Using Your Gifts
- Consider Your Past
- Consider What Gives You Joy and Satisfaction
- Ask Others for Their Opinions
- Consider the Needs You Observe
- Experiment in Using Your Gifts
- Obey Christ's Commission and Commands
- Stretch Yourself
- Realize You Have the Potential for Any Gift
- Rejoice in the Lord

174

III. How to Use Your Gifts With Love 1 Cor. 13.
- The Value of Love 1 Cor. 13:1-3
- The Virtues of Love 1 Cor. 13:4-8
- The Victory of Love 1 Cor. 13:8-13

Chapter Nine

Discovering and Using Your Gifts with Love

Knowing what your spiritual gifts are can be an asset to your spiritual life and your service to Christ. It can help you build the confidence you need to serve Him. You can develop and strengthen your spiritual gifts by equipping yourself to use them better.

The question is, "How can a person know what his or her gifts are?"

As I mentioned at the beginning of this book, the popular method today is to use a "spiritual gifts evaluation form," a "spiritual gifts inventory", or a "spiritual gifts questionnaire." The problem is that while filling out and discussing these is enjoyable, and while having an emphasis on gifts is healthy, such inventories are inadequate to serve as a guide for our spiritual lives and service. They are subjective rather than objective in their analysis. When a person fills out the questionnaire, he or she can slant answers to manipulate the result so it will be what the person has predetermined it to be. The conclusions can be affected by a person's unconscious desire to have a particular gift or distaste for a ministry that involves other gifts.

In the *Journal of Psychology and Theology*; 1994; Vol. 22; No. 1; pp. 39-44 in an article entitled *Spiritual Gifts: A Psychometric Extension*, Stewart E. Cooper, Valparaiso University, and Stephen D. Blakeman, O'Berry Center, reported an examination of spiritual gifts inventories using rigorous test standardization methods. Their observation was as follows: "Spiritual gifts inventories appear to be constructed in a scientific manner, but they are often technically inadequate. The current study of the Objective Questionnaire Testing set of the Motivational Spiritual Gifts Inventory (MGI). Analysis of the questionnaire data indicated that despite the apparent strength of the spiritual gifts subscales' content validity, reliability fell only in the poor to moderate range. Construct validity was also tenuous."

If spiritual gifts inventories are not a reliable approach to take to discover a person's gifts, then how can we detect which ones we have? How can we know our gifts?" The important question is, "What does God want me to do?" Whatever He wants me to do, He will enable me to accomplish. Obedience is the key!

HOW ARE YOU RELATING TO YOUR GIFTS?

Believers differ in the ways they relate to the issue of their spiritual gifts and how they use them. How do you relate to the fact that you have spiritual gifts? Do you feel a sense of responsibility for using them? Do you think you are accountable to God for what you do with them? Let us examine the ways some believers are treating their gifts. How are they being used?

1. Some Are Unaware of Gifts

Some believers have no knowledge at all of gifts. Some do not know they have gifts. Many of these are spiritually and emotionally immature. Some have a low spiritual self-esteem. They do not think they can do anything to serve their Lord.

These need to be taught the Word of God and challenged to obey Him in witness and ministry.

As they grow in Christ, they will begin to pray and seek to obey the commission of Christ. The Holy Spirit will surface gifts in their lives. This will be a tremendous encouragement to their lives as they begin to realize their gifts and find joy in serving Christ.

2. Some Are Withholding Their Gifts

Some unfaithful servants are sinfully withholding their gifts from our Lord and His Body. These have become self-centered rather than Christ-centered. They are like the man in our Lord's parable who fearfully hid his talent in the earth.

These unfaithful believers need spiritual renewal in their lives. They need to experience a fresh touch and a new joy that comes from walking in obedience to Christ. Spiritual leaders and other members of the Body need to minister to these to enlist, equip, engage, and encourage them in witness and ministry for Christ.

3. Some Are Misusing Their Gifts

Some are prostituting their gifts. They are "selling-out" themselves and their gifts to the world and the devil, who pays with prestige, power, position, and money for the use of their gifts. Satan makes attractive offers to these people to divert the use of their gifts from where God wants to use them into using them for self or for evil. The unfaithful allow their gifts to be bought by the evil one rather than giving them in love as the bride of Christ to their Lord.

A church I where I was pastor was in a major relocation and building program. It was a very demanding project. We put the organization together carefully. One of our businessmen had shown in his business and in his leadership in the church that he had the gift of administration. He was chosen as our building-committee chairman. He worked tirelessly for a period of five years leading in the building program. During that time he could have made much money if he had concentrated the extra efforts and leadership he gave to the Lord's work into his own business. God blessed and used him, but he could have prostituted his gifts and used them sinfully for the devil and for himself.

Many believers do not honor and serve God with their gifts. They need to repent and submit to the Father to use every gift for His glory.

4. Some Are Discovering Their Gifts

Some are in the process of discovering gifts. Every member of the church has at least one gift, probably more than one. But many are like I was as a young Christian. I did not think I had any gift with which to serve God. Through the encouragement of my pastor, church, parents, and the work of the Holy Spirit, God taught me that He had endowed me with gifts. As I began to serve, gifts began to surface. God had been preparing me for the time when He would begin to use these gifts within the Body of Christ. Every Christian needs to be affirmed and challenged to discover the gifts God has placed in their lives.

5. Some Are Developing Their Gifts

Some are developing the gifts with which God has endowed them. They are conscientiously training and equipping themselves to use their gifts in witness and ministry for our Lord. They are growing and maturing through the exercise of their gifts. Church leaders can do no better than to assist each member in discovering and developing the gifts for ministry God has given them.

6. Some Are Dynamically Using Their Gifts

Many are using their gifts to build up the Body of Christ and to glorify Him. A church can never reach its potential with a "hired staff" mentality. The church's hope of reaching and ministering to people is the ministry of the laity. A mighty army of believers must be enlisted, equipped, and engaged in the mighty work of ministry and witness. The hope of reaching our world for Christ is through lay volunteers, bi-vocational pastors, and leaders being available to God to go wherever they are needed in the name of Christ.

HOW YOU CAN DISCOVER YOUR GIFTS

God does not play games. He created us! He has a mission for each of us! God wants us to know Him and how to live for and serve Him. The problem is not God's inability to communicate His will and reveal His plan to us. The problem is our inability and unwillingness to receive what God has for us. We can take 10 steps to can help us know and effectively use our gifts.

1. Pray for God's Direction for Using Your Gifts

Prayer is central in living the life God has for us to live! He reveals His will to us as we earnestly and fervently seek His face. God responds to a seeking heart. God promised, "Call to Me, and I will answer you, and show you great and mighty things, which you do not know" (Jer. 33:2). He desires to reveal His will to us including what our gifts are and how we can use them effectively. He has shown us His love and concern so we can know how to be in a position to receive all He has for us. "For I know the thoughts that I think toward you, says the Lord, thoughts of peace and not of evil, to give you a future and a hope. Then you will call upon Me and go and pray to Me, and I will listen to you. And you will seek Me and find Me, when you search for Me with all your heart" (Jer. 29:11-13).

Earnest and sincere prayer will bring us to a spirit of humility and repentance. When we are broken and yielded to Him, we become available to serve Him wherever and however He desires. Then, He will surface the gift we need to serve and glorify Him.

2. Consider Your Past

Recall the successful things you did as a child. They can show trends toward gifts that are in your life. Remember the subjects in school where you excelled and the tasks for which you were trained. Think about the ways you have been successful in business or on your job. Make a list of the ways you have served Christ through your church, by ministering to individuals, and by helping in your community. A consideration of your past involvement will serve as an indicator of what your gifts may be.

3. Consider What Gives You Joy and Satisfaction

We enjoy and find satisfaction in doing the things we do well. When we seem to fit the particular job or place of service, it indicates that we have a gift in that area of ministry. What we do well is an indicator of our gifts. We will find joy through using the spiritual gift our Lord has given us.

4. Ask Others for Their Opinions and Counsel

Seek the opinions and counsel of people who know you. Family, friends, acquaintances, and others who observe us are helpful in assessing our gift potential. Many times they can offer objective input to help us better understand what we can do and how effective we are. Especially seek the counsel of those who will be candid and honest with you, even when it may be emotionally difficult to accept. A friend who has the gift of mercy might be more affirming than you need to accurately assess your gifts. A person who is a wise leader may help. A friend with a gift of discernment or administration would be a good possibility.

5. Consider Needs You Observe

Needs are everywhere. You will not see them all. You will perceive and be concerned about some of them. The needs you observe tell something about you. They may well serve partially as another indicator of what your spiritual gift is. The fact that you see a need could indicate that God wants to use you to meet it. As you attempt to do so, the gift to do it may surface.

6. Experiment in Using Your Gifts

Try something new and different by involving yourself in activities, projects, and ministries you have never done. It may surface a latent gift within you that you did not know you had. God has outstanding possibilities for each of us. It is a tremendous adventure to trust God and attempt things for His glory we have never done before.

Ed was a businessman in charge of sales for his company. He occasionally came to Sunday School but did not enjoy it. He told his wife it was a waste of time to listen to the teacher read from his teacher's book. One Sunday the teacher had to be away. The director asked Ed to teach that Sunday. Ed replied, "I am no teacher, but I will do it!

Ed did it! And they kept on asking him to do it. Soon, he was the regular teacher. The class grew until it filled and overflowed its meeting place. Next, they asked him to lead the church's training program. This would require the use of the gift of administration/leadership. Ed said, "I will do it under two conditions. One, if all the deacons and leaders will attend and participate. Two, if you will give me three minutes at the beginning of the evening worship service." The church leaders agreed. Every Sunday evening Ed got a different leader to take the three minutes to promote the training program. The training program grew until it filled the church building on Sunday nights. By being willing to experiment Ed discovered that he had a gift to teach.

7. Obey Christ's Commission and Commands

Jesus is Lord! We are His servants. As a believer simply obeys Christ, his gifts will surface. Our Lord's command is that we love one another. If we love one another, we will try to do what is needed. God will enable us to be of help in some way. His commission is that we share Christ with every person. As obey Him by loving people and sharing Christ with them, God will surface the gifts needed to accomplish what He told us to do.

8. Stretch Yourself

The life of obedience to Christ is a terrific adventure. Place your hand in His and walk with Him. Determine that you will attempt anything that needs to be done for His glory and to reach people. Don't cop out! Don't find an excuse not to use a particular gift. Don't avoid any of the gifts. Be willing for God to work through you using any gift He chooses to use. Try all the gifts! Develop their use in your life as God leads you.

9. Realize You Have the Potential for Any Gift

You have the potential for any gift through Christ who lives in you. Jesus is the perfect person. He is the possessor of every gift. He lives in you! It "is Christ in you, the hope of glory" (Col. 1:27). Since the one who lives in you possesses every gift, then you do have the potential for any gift through Him. The Holy Spirit will surface whatever gift you need to obey Him in witness and ministry through His power that is at work in you. Along with Paul, you can rightfully say, "I can do all things through Christ who strengthens me" (Phil. 4:13).

10. Rejoice in the Lord and Totally Obey Christ

Praise God for the joy of His purpose. Praise Him for His using you. Give Him thanks in everything. Be grateful for God's gifts to you and for the way He has chosen to use you. Let the grace of the

Lord Jesus Christ flow through you to others. "The joy of the Lord is your strength" (Neh. 8:10). Let the joy of the Lord be your strength in your usage of your gifts and in witness and ministry for Christ.

Be humbly and gratefully available to Him 24 hours every day, seven days a week. Be ready to go wherever and whenever He leads you to go in service for His glory. God is seeking people like this to bless and use. The bottom line in knowing our gifts is to obey Christ. What He engages us to do, He enables us to do.

The bottom line is obedience! Obedience is the key to carrying out the will of God! Obedience is the key for discovering your spiritual gifts! Obedience is the key to the surfacing of your gift!

HOW TO USE YOUR GIFT WITH LOVE

Every gift is secondary to love. Every biblical passage about gifts is set in the context of an admonition to love. Gifts become effective as they are permeated with God's "more excellent way."

In Romans 12:6, 9-10 an admonition is given to use your gifts with love, "Having then gifts differing according to the grace that is given to us, let us use them: if prophecy, let us prophesy in proportion to our faith; . . . Let love be without hypocrisy. Abhor what is evil. Cling to what is good. Be kindly affectionate to one another with brotherly love, in honor giving preference to one another."

After the gift passage in Ephesians 4:11-12 is the strong emphasis on love, "But speaking the truth in love, may grow up in all things into Him who is the head—Christ—from whom the whole body, joined and knit together by what every joint supplies, according to the effective working by which every part does its share, causes growth of the body for the edifying of itself in love" (Eph. 4:15-16).

The longest Body-life chapter, 1 Corinthians 12, ends with a list of powerful gifts and concludes by shocking the readers in Corinth who elevated their spiritual gifts with great pride. 1 Corinthians 12:31 admonishes, "But earnestly desire the best gifts. And, yet I show you a more excellent way." Then, comes the magnificent revelation on the greatest gift, Chapter 13. Self-centered Corinthians had gotten themselves into a quagmire of controversy. Paul pointed the way out.

"Way" translates *hodon*, a road. "More excellent" translates *hyper-bolen*, something beyond comparison, super, or greater than.

Paul pointed the way out of the quagmire to the super highway of the "God-kind-of-love" (*agape*). No matter what spiritual gift you have, if it is to have validity with God, it must be exercised in Christian love.

This love is special! It is not sexual love (*eros*). It is not love denoting friendship—brotherly love (*philos*). It is the highest kind of love, the God-kind-of-love (agape). It is the love that gives itself. It is the John 3:16 kind of love

1. The Value Of Love (I Cor. 13:1-3)

Love is superior to "tongues" or "languages." Paul started here, not because it was the most important gift but because of the undue emphasis placed on tongues. The most poetic, logical, eloquent speech is not enough. Words must be spoken in love, not in egotistical exhibition.

Love is superior to the gifts of prophecy, understanding, knowledge, and faith. "Prophecy" denotes powerful preaching. "Understanding" may go to the extent of the person's receiving divine revelation that exceeds all human reason. A person may have "all knowledge" or have faith that is truly mountain-moving. But, the person with all of these highest attributes is "nothing" without love. He or she is just one big zero without love!

2. The Virtues of Love (1 Cor. 13:4-8)

Love expresses itself through attitudes and actions. It reveals itself through our behavior! The attributes in 1 Corinthians 13 could describe only one person—**Jesus.** The virtues are listed in verses 4-8.

Love "suffers long." It is patient, even tempered, continues with steadfast endurance. No one treated Abraham Lincoln with more contempt than did Edwin M. Stanton, his rival. He called Lincoln a "low cunning clown." He nicknamed him the "original gorilla." Stanton said, "There is no need for a circus to search all over Africa for a gorilla when you could find one so easily in Springfield, Illinois."

Lincoln said nothing. When he became president, he made Stanton his Secretary of War because he was the best person for the job. He treated Stanton with every courtesy. When Lincoln was murdered by the assassin's bullet, Stanton stood over the coffin and said with tears, "There lies the greatest ruler of men the world has ever seen."

Love is "kind." Love knows gentleness and kindness, not severity and harshness. Those who are not very kind are not very holy.

Love does not "envy." It is not jealous. It finds no joy in seeing others fail. Envy is the curse of religion.

Selfish ambition always begrudges those who fare well.

Love does not "parade itself." Love does not brag. Bragging proceeds from the idea of superiority over others. Love is kept humble by the consciousness that it can never offer its loved one a gift that is good enough. God in His love gave us His best.

Love is not "puffed up." It is not inflated with its own ego. It is not self-important, filled with pride and conceit.

Love "does not behave rudely." Love is not graceless. It is filled with charm. It is courteous, not blunt and brutal. A professor said of a student, "Let him go where he will, his face will be a sermon in itself."

Love "does not seek its own." It does not insist upon its own rights. It does not demand to have its own way. Love thinks of its duties rather than its rights. Love has given its rights to Jesus.

Love "is not provoked." It does not fly into a temper nor wear its feelings on its shirtsleeve.

It doesn't take exception to things and is not touchy or sensitive. Love thinks the best of all.

Love "thinks no evil." It does not store up the memory of wrongs it has received. It does not keep an accountant's ledger of the ways it has been mistreated. Love forgives and forgets. It is said that the Polynesians kept articles in their huts to remind themselves of their hate for their enemies. They nursed their wrath to keep it warm.

Love "does not rejoice in iniquity." It finds no pleasure in evil doing. It does not enjoy hearing of others' misfortunes. Love does not want to hear a spicy story that discredits someone. Love can not only weep with those who weep, but it can rejoice with those who rejoice.

Love "rejoices in truth." It has no desire to veil the truth. It is brave enough to face the truth because it has nothing to hide. The truth sets us free.

Love "bears all things." It can go on in spite of insult, injury, or disappointment. Love would much rather set about quietly mending things than publicly rebuking them.

Love "believes all things." It is completely trusting. In relation to God, it takes God at His Word. In relation to others—it is not suspicious. Love believes the best about others.

Love "hopes all things." It never gives up hope. Jesus never saw any person as hopeless. The Gadarean demoniac was not hopeless to Jesus. Adam Clark was one of the great theologians. When Clark was a boy, a distinguished visitor came to his school. The teacher singled out Adam Clark as "the stupidest boy in the school." Before he left the school the visitor came to Adam Clark and said, "Never mind, my boy, you may be a great scholar some day. Don't be discouraged, but try hard, and keep on trying." He gave a word of hope.

Love "endures all things." Love lasts to the end. Others may stop, but love keeps on. All these qualities of love we see actualized in the life of Jesus Christ. All these qualities may be found in our lives as we lose our lives in Christ Jesus.

3. The Victory of Love (1 Cor. 13:8-13)

Love never fails—it lasts! The greatest gifts and the most popular gifts will fade away (v. 8).

There will be a time when we are with Christ in heaven. There will be no need for these gifts when we are with Him.

Love brings us to maturity (v. 10-12). Love brings us to the time when we see Him as He is. We will be with Him and be like Him.

Love abides throughout eternity (v. 13). Faith, hope, and love abide, but the greatest of these is love.

Our present faith will have become sight. Our present hope (assurance) will have become realization. They will still abide along with love. Love is the source of faith and hope. Without God's love we would have no faith nor hope. Love is the greatest of all graces or gifts. It is the very nature of God Himself. God is love.

The greatest adventure you can know is to simply place your hand in the hand of Jesus, walk in obedience to Him, and let Him permeate your life with His love. Then, use every gift in obedience for His glory.

ACTIVITIES

1. How are you treating your gifts?

_____ Unaware of them?   _____ Withholding them?
_____ Misusing them?   _____ Discovering them?
_____ Developing them?   _____ Dynamically using them?

2. List three actions you can take that will help you discover your spiritual gifts.

1. _____

2. _____

3. _____

3. What gift do you know in your heart that you have but that you have not had the courage to stretch yourself to try?

_____

4. Did the Holy Spirit surface the gift in your life?
Yes _____ No _____

5. What is the bottom line in knowing and using your gifts?

_____

_____

_____

6. What is superior to all gifts?

_____

7. Examine your own life and list the virtues of love from 1 Corinthians 13:4-8 that are present in your life.

_____

_____

_____

_____

_____

Order other books from Hannibal Books

Rescue by Jean Phillips. Abducted and threatened with death, this Baptist missionary and her husband draw on God's lessons of a lifetime. Walk with this inspiring couple through those harrrowing years when they were literally refined by the African fires blazing around them.

_____ **Copies at $12.95 =** _____

It's a Jungle Out There (Book 1 of the Rani series) "Conceived in the Amazon rain forest, I learned to walk and talk among the Machiguenga Indians who, to this day, call me Rani," writes Snell. "As they touched our lives, we discovered what it would cost to touch theirs."

_____ **Copies at $7.95 =** _____

Life is a Jungle (Book 2 of the Rani series) "I never thought it unusual to have a 16-foot anaconda slithering around in our science class. Or going barefoot to school, getting stuck in the middle of landslides or getting cheap thrills careening through the streets of Lima in taxis," writes Snell.

_____ **Copies at $7.95 =** _____

Jungle Calls (Book 3 of the Rani series) "Standing in inky black jungle, we were hundreds of miles from the nearest light bulb. The call of insects and frogs shrilled in our ears. Somewhere nearby, we knew, were Indians who killed anyone who ventured into their territory," writes Snell.

_____ **Copies at $7.95 =** _____

Please add $3.00 postage and handling for first book, plus 50-cents for each additional book.

Shipping & Handling _____
TX residents add sales tax _____
TOTAL ENCLOSED _____

check _____ or credit card# _____ exp. date_____

(Visa, MasterCard, Discover, American Express accepted)

Name _____

Address _____

City _____ State _____ Zip _____

MAIL TO: HANNIBAL BOOKS,
P.O. BOX 461592,
Garland, TX 75046
OR CALL: 1-800-747-0738